CHASING BATS
AND
TRACKING RATS

Urban Ecology, Community Science, and How We Share Our Cities

written by
CYLITA GUY

illustrations by
CORNELIA LI

annick
press
toronto · berkeley

To my parents, who helped a Black,
city kid grow up with a deep love of nature.
I hope this book helps other melanated kids do the same.
—C.G.

Cover art by Cornelia Li, designed by Paul Covello
Interior designed by Paul Covello and Danielle Arbour
Edited by Claire Caldwell
Copyedited by Debbie Innes
Proofread by Doeun Rivendell
Indexed by Wendy Thomas

Annick Press Ltd.

We acknowledge the support of the Canada Council for the Arts and the
Ontario Arts Council, and the participation of the Government of Canada/la
participation du gouvernement du Canada for our publishing activities.

ONTARIO ARTS COUNCIL
CONSEIL DES ARTS DE L'ONTARIO
an Ontario government agency
un organisme du gouvernement de l'Ontario

Library and Archives Canada Cataloguing in Publication

Title: Chasing bats and tracking rats : urban ecology, community science, and how we share our
cities / written by Cylita Guy ; illustrations by Cornelia Li.
Names: Guy, Cylita, author. | Li, Cornelia, illustrator.
Identifiers: Canadiana (print) 20210188731 | Canadiana (ebook) 20210188758 | ISBN 9781773215396
(softcover) | ISBN 9781773215389 (hardcover) | ISBN 9781773215419 (PDF) | ISBN 9781773215402
(HTML)
Subjects: LCSH: Urban ecology (Biology)—Juvenile literature. | LCSH: Urban animals—Juvenile
literature.
Classification: LCC QH541.5.C6 G89 2021 | DDC j577.5/6—dc23

Published in the U.S.A. by Annick Press (U.S.) Ltd.
Distributed in Canada by University of Toronto Press.
Distributed in the U.S.A. by Publishers Group West.

Printed in China

annickpress.com
cylitaguy.com
corneliali.com

Also available as an e-book. Please visit annickpress.com/ebooks for more details.

INTRODUCTION
Living in the Urban Jungle

There are more than seven billion people on earth. Over half of these people (around 55 percent) live in cities. That's a lot! And guess what? That number keeps going up. Cities may make life easier for many humans by bringing us closer to things like grocery stores, jobs, and hospitals, but they make it much harder for most wildlife.

Think about it—to build our cities we destroy the natural spaces that are homes for insects, plants, and animals. We make roadways that split forests into smaller pieces. We mow fields so we have parks to play in. Sometimes we even get rid of everything when we pave over the ground to create parking lots. These changes are too much for many plants and animals to handle. Without the right type of habitat, many species can't survive in cities. This means there is often less biodiversity—or different types of plants and animals—in cities compared to natural spaces.

But guess what? Some creatures seem to do okay in cities. In fact, some species do better in cities than in their natural habitats! There is still a lot we don't know about urban wildlife, but scientists are learning more every day. As cities continue to grow and expand, it's important that we understand how city living may be changing the behavior of these species and how living so close to them may be affecting us.

The scientists who study how different species interact with each other and their environments are called ecologists. When most people think of these wildlife scientists, they think of people adventuring in far-off places. Perhaps you've even seen ecologists like these on TV—diving in the ocean or exploring in rainforests. But there is a whole group of ecologists who study the animals and plants living in cities! Ecologists like me. Hi! My name is Cylita and I'm one of the many urban ecologists around the world helping us understand nature in our cities.

Have you ever wondered how far rats scurrying out of dumpsters might travel in the city? Or how many bird species are in your local park? What about the ways that plants can fight climate change in urban areas?

From bats to bees and microplastics to trees, this book will introduce you to urban ecologists who answer questions like these ones. And because science requires teamwork, all of the urban ecologists you'll meet are people that I know and have worked with!

You'll also learn about the wacky ways we do our science in urban environments (like riding a science bike!). Cities are complicated and busy places filled with lots of different challenges to doing research. As urban ecologists, we have to come up with creative approaches to get our data and build cool tools to help answer our questions. Some of my urban ecologist friends even get everyday people—like you!—to help them collect their data.

We want to help you understand why nature is so important in our cities. Humans get a lot of benefits—or ecosystem services—from nature, but we also have a responsibility to keep our environments healthy and protect the species living in them. We also want you to explore your own local biodiversity, so keep an eye out for urban ecology challenges at the end of each chapter. Who knows, while you're out adventuring in your neighborhood, you might even meet one of us—or your own friendly neighborhood urban ecologist!

URBAN ECOLOGY CHALLENGE

Each scientist in this book has created a challenge just for you! These challenges will get you thinking like an urban ecologist, and will show you how to be a protector of your local biodiversity. Before you start, make sure you have a small notebook and pencil. No explorer, adventurer, or scientist goes anywhere without their trusty field notebook!

Look, but don't touch (and please don't feed!)

Throughout this book, you're going to hear stories from scientists who catch and handle wildlife for a living. These scientists—me included—have had years of training and wear special equipment to keep them and the animals they handle safe. When you go out to enjoy the species in your neighborhood, please don't try to touch any of the animals you meet! And don't share your food with them. Although lots of animals beg for human treats, this food can make them sick later.

TALK LIKE AN URBAN ECOLOGIST!
Key Terms

Here are a few special terms we urban ecologists use in our work—terms that will pop up in many chapters in this book. If you're reading and aren't sure what a word means, flip back to this page.

Urban
Also known as cities, urban areas are places where lots of people live and work together.

Suburban
As you move toward the outskirts of cities, homes and people usually become more spread out. These are called suburban areas.

Rural
Outside of cities, people may live in small groups surrounded by farmland and natural areas. These are rural communities.

Wilderness
These are natural areas that haven't been changed by humans, or where human activity is minimal.

Ecosystem services
The benefits humans receive from natural environments and the species inhabiting them. For example, animals and insects pollinate our crops; trees and other plants provide building materials (not to mention the air we breathe!); and wetlands help to filter and purify water.

Hypothesis

Science is all about asking questions about the way the world works. A hypothesis is a well-thought-out answer to a question we have asked, but haven't yet tested with an experiment or through observation. To come up with hypotheses, we often need to do research to get enough information to make a statement about what we think will happen.

Let's say we want to know if plants grow larger when they have access to sunlight. If we did some research, we would find out that plants use the sun's energy to produce their food through photosynthesis. Based on this, we could hypothesize that if a plant is given no light, it won't grow.

Experiment

Once we have asked a question and come up with a hypothesis, we can design an experiment to test it.

To find out if sunlight makes plants grow, we could design an experiment with two plants on a windowsill. We could cover one plant with a box so it gets no light and leave the other uncovered. Since we are only interested in the effect of sunlight, we would want to make sure that nothing else differs between our plants. This means we'd have to use the same species of plant, give them the same amount of water at the same time, and keep them at the same temperature.

Observation

While experiments are an important part of science, most of the urban ecologists you'll meet in this book are trying to make observations about nature in cities (but many urban ecologists do experiments, too). Observation means watching the natural world to understand patterns and see what might change over time. With observational science, we don't manipulate or change anything like we would with an experiment.

For example, if we wanted to know the height of the average middle school student living in Fredericton, New Brunswick, in Canada we couldn't answer this question by doing an experiment. Instead, we would need to go out and make some observations about Fredericton's middle schoolers.

Sampling

When scientists try to make observations about patterns in the world, we can't always measure everything. Instead, we collect information from a smaller part of a population, landscape, or natural process that we want to measure. This is called sampling.

It would be very hard and take a lot of time to measure the height of every single sixth grader in Fredericton, so we might choose to measure the heights of children in classrooms from three different schools across the city. This sample of sixth graders should give us an idea of the overall pattern of heights in all of Fredericton.

Data

Data is all the information we collect and record while sampling or conducting an experiment. With our plant experiment, our data might be daily measurements of the height of each plant. With our sixth graders, it would be measurements of each kid's height. A dataset is a collection of all the data that comes from an experiment or project.

Bias

Bias is a preference for one thing, group, or location over others. Sometimes datasets can be biased toward, or contain only information on, certain groups of people or things because we aren't careful with how we design our experiments or sampling. When our experiments or observations are biased, we can miss important pieces of information that will affect the answers to the questions we ask.

If we measured the heights of only sixth-grade students in Fredericton, our sample would be biased toward sixth graders. We wouldn't be able to use our data to say something about the heights of all middle school students in the city because we wouldn't have height information for the seventh- and eighth-grade students also at the school. To avoid bias, we'd want to measure students from all grades from several middle schools in different neighborhoods so that our sample is representative of the whole population.

Processing

A process is a series of related actions or steps that scientists take to get to an outcome. In urban ecology, processing refers to the steps we take to collect data when we are sampling individual animals, plants, or people in a population.

Many types of information can be collected during processing. An ecologist might want to know how old an animal is, how heavy it is, and its sex (male or female). They might collect several different samples from an individual, including fur, blood, or urine. They might also want to tag the animal or plant so they can identify it later.

Processing the Fredericton sixth graders might involve taking their names (so we know who we've measured), measuring their heights, and recording what school they were from.

Results

Results are the end or outcome of an experiment or sampling. In the plant experiment, the result would be seeing which plant (the one with light or the one without) grew taller. In the example with our sixth graders, the result would be the average height calculated from the data we collected.

CHAPTER 1
CHASING DOWN BIG BROWNS
How much do wildlife rely on city green spaces?

I BET THE LAST TIME YOU PLAYED AT THE PARK, you saw some wildlife sharing it with you. Birds in trees. Squirrels running around. Turtles sunning themselves on rocks in a pond. Parks and green spaces are often the closest thing to the natural habitats of animals and plants in urban environments. So, we like to think of them as being good habitat for wildlife in the city. That's what I thought when I set out to study city bats in High Park—a large green space in Toronto, Canada. It seemed like the perfect habitat for city bats. High Park is full of tall old trees that bats might like to sleep in. It also has a large pond that bats could forage—or hunt—for insects.

But after chasing bats around the park all summer, I'd barely caught any. Where were the bats going at night to feed? Where were they sleeping during the day? It didn't seem like bats were using the park at all. But I was about to learn—in the most dangerous way possible—that this wasn't quite the case . . .

WHO'S afraid OF a BIG BROWN Bat?

"The park is closed. What are you still doing here?"

Pausing, I looked up at the large, grumpy police officer standing in front of the picnic table I was sitting at. Around me were a number of strange items: test tubes for storing samples, a margarine container full of measuring tapes, a pile of tiny felt bags, and a kitchen scale. Beside me sat Krista, my bat-catching partner in crime. She and I were now several hours into processing the 25 bats we had caught in the chimney of a nearby house.

I sighed. It was one o'clock in the morning and it had already been a very long night. Earlier that evening, Krista had climbed a ladder and dangled herself and our roost trap over the side of a four-story home. After searching all summer, we'd finally found our first bat colony in a neighborhood filled with large old houses and trees—just a few blocks away from High Park. The people living there had given us permission to climb on the roof that night.

TOOLS OF THE TRADE

Usually I use mist nets to catch bats while they are out flying at night. Mist nets are like big, fine-mesh fishing nets that we put high up in the air between two poles. These nets are split into sections (called tiers) with baggy pockets at the bottom. Unsuspecting bats fly into these nets and get tangled in those pockets. Before starting my processing, I carefully untangle them, making sure they aren't hurt.

When we need to catch bats in areas where there are too many trees or the ground is too hard to put up a mist net, we use harp traps instead. Harp traps are made of a big metal square with fishing line looped around it. Bats try to fly through the fishing line, get caught, and then fall into a bag at the bottom. The roost trap Krista used to catch bats as they left the chimney for the night was a lighter and smaller version of a harp trap.

But the easiest way to catch a bat is when they're roosting in an area that we can get into (like a cave or an attic). Then we can just go up with a gloved hand and pick them off the walls!

As the sun set, I had watched excitedly from a lower section of the roof as our trap filled with bats.

After an hour, Krista had lowered a bag full of squirming bats into my arms! I had almost squealed at the thought of how much data we were going to be able to collect from them. Everything had been going perfectly, until it had come time for Krista to get down from the roof. As Krista stepped onto the first rung of the ladder—she slipped.

Krista had fallen from the ladder and tumbled toward the edge of the roof! But I had jumped forward and grabbed her by the belt just before she fell off. Thinking about it again had my heart racing. Krista's near-death experience had been stressful enough, and now, the police officer shining his light in my face was giving me a headache.

"Ma'am," the police officer said, snapping me back to the present, "please answer my question. What are you doing in the park?"

I explained that I was a scientist who studied bats living in cities. I told the officer about the 25 bats we'd caught and how we had brought them to the park so we could collect information about them before letting them go.

The police officer nodded and asked if he could see one of my bats. I held up my gloved hand. Inside my closed palm, a tiny brown face squirmed, trying to escape. "It's a big brown bat, but they really aren't that big!" I joked. The officer didn't laugh.

"Where are the rest of the bats?" he asked. "Have you let them go already?"

I told him that we hadn't yet because it was so cold. Even though it was a summer night, it was only 10 degrees Celsius (50 degrees Fahrenheit). When bats get cold, they go into a hibernation-like state called torpor. Because they've dropped their body temperature to save energy, torpid bats are slow and sluggish—and they can't fly. I explained that we had to warm up all our bats before we could let them go.

The officer's eyes got larger and larger, until finally he put up his hand to stop me. "Ma'am," he said, squinting. "Do you know that your shirt is moving?"

I looked down. Sure enough, there were several squeaking lumps wiggling around between my sweater and T-shirt. "Of course, officer!" I grinned. "Like I was saying, we have to warm our bats back up. So, the rest of the colony is down my shirt and under my armpit. And it looks like some of them are just about ready to start flying again!"

The police officer shook his head and took off pretty fast.

Bats are not rats

Ever heard that bats are just flying rats with wings? Not true! While both bats and rodents are mammals, bats are their own separate group, Chiroptera. Chiroptera comes from the Greek words *chiro*, meaning hand, and *ptera*, meaning wing. So, Chiroptera literally means "hand wing."

Some other common bat myths debunked: bats won't get stuck in your hair when they're out flying, they aren't blind, and not all species are blood feeders.

WHY DO We Care aBOUT CITY BaTS?

Bats get a bad rep. Maybe it's because there are lots of bat stories and myths that scare people—like that police officer. Maybe it's because they're often found living in people's attics and chimneys and are considered pests. But just like every species, bats are important parts of our ecosystems. Many bats eat insects, helping to keep their populations in check. Some of these insects are pests that feed on our crops—which include your backyard or community garden. In warmer places, bats also pollinate flowers (like bees and birds do) and help disperse seeds. Because they perform so many services for our environment, it's important that we understand what they need to survive both in and outside of cities.

Scientists have a good idea of what types of bats we can find in cities around the world. But we don't have as good of an idea about how they move through urban landscapes or how they change their behavior when they're here. This is why I risked life and limb to find out more about Toronto's bats!

Let's talk about diversity!

Bats are the only mammals capable of true powered flight. This means they don't just glide (like flying squirrels) but they actually generate the force needed to get off the ground and stay in the air (like birds, insects, and extinct pterosaurs, a type of flying reptile).

There are more than 1,400 species of bats worldwide, making them the second-most species-rich group of mammals on Earth! Bats live everywhere except in the High Arctic and Antarctica, where it's too cold for them. Most bat species eat insects, some eat fruit, and others feed on nectar from flowers. Some even eat fish, birds, mice, and other animals. There are three species of bats that feed only on blood—the vampire bats!

WHERE DO CITY BATS GO TO SLEEP?

Because I thought High Park was good bat habitat, I had a couple of hypotheses when I started my sampling. First, I thought I would catch more adult female bats than adult male bats. Female bats need access to the best areas in the landscape to make sure they get enough food. They need lots of energy to raise their babies. I also thought I would find both male and female bats foraging in the park at night and roosting—or sleeping—in it during the day.

Every night from June to September, I went out to catch bats in the park. I would stay up from sunset to sunrise and sleep during the day, just like the bats I was studying. For every bat that I caught, I collected information on their age, weight, size, and whether they were male or female. So that I could tell my bats apart, I used a needle to put a small microchip with a unique ID under their skin. (Vets do this to our pets, too!) Every time I caught a bat, I scanned for this microchip to see if it was one I'd caught before. Finally, I glued a small radio-tag to the backs of some of these bats. These radio-tags emitted beeps that I could hear using a large antenna and receiver. At night, I would listen for these beeps to figure out where the bats were feeding. I would also follow the beeps during the day to see where they'd gone to sleep.

Picking up bat echolocation calls

Many bat species echolocate to help them find their food and their way around. Bats that echolocate send high-frequency sound waves into the environment. These sound waves bounce off objects, creating an "echo" that returns to bats' ears, letting them know where those objects are in space. Bat echolocation calls are outside the range of human hearing. But we can use special tools, called acoustic bat detectors, to turn these bat sounds into a noise we can hear.

Depending on where you live, your city may have a bat monitoring program that lets you borrow acoustic detectors to help collect information on local bats. For example, in the United Kingdom, people can sign up to help collect acoustic data with the Bat Conservation Trust's National Bat Monitoring Programme.

WHAT IF CITY BATS DON'T LIKE GREEN SPACES AS MUCH AS WE THINK?

Do you know what all that data told me? The exact opposite of what I'd expected! Most of the bats I caught in High Park were males—not females. When I did catch female bats, it was only in areas closest to the largest body of water. We tracked most of these females back to the colony in the chimney that I told you about earlier.

None of the bats I radio-tagged roosted in the park. Instead, I found them sleeping in people's homes or in trees in their backyards. And most of the bats I radio-tagged seemed to only feed in the park for part of the night before disappearing. All of this data suggests that High Park— what seemed like bat paradise—isn't actually the best habitat for them.

Not just for the birds . . .

Want to do something to promote good bat habitat in your backyard? Try putting up a bat house! Bat houses are shelters where bats can roost during the day. It's a lot like a bird house, except the hole is in the bottom. Bats may not always form large colonies in the house you put up, but they may still use it for a night's rest here and there!

This doesn't mean High Park is bad for bats. Bats are still using the park, just not as much as I thought. It seems like they come to the park early in the evening, feed for a little bit, and then

Where in the world?

At 399 acres, High Park seems big while you're walking through it. After all, you could fit about 302 American football fields inside of it! But there are much bigger city parks across the world, like Stanley Park in Vancouver (1,000 acres or 757 football fields), the Staten Island Green Belt in New York (2,800 acres or 2,121 football fields), and Bois de Boulogne in Paris (2,100 acres or more than 1,500 football fields).

go somewhere else in the city for the rest of the night. But I don't know where these bats are going to feed . . . yet. I could go out again another summer to try and track where they're going. That would be a step toward figuring out which urban green spaces are best for bats, and what about their design makes them so good. This information can help us protect habitat for bats living in cities and design our green spaces to be better for bats in the future.

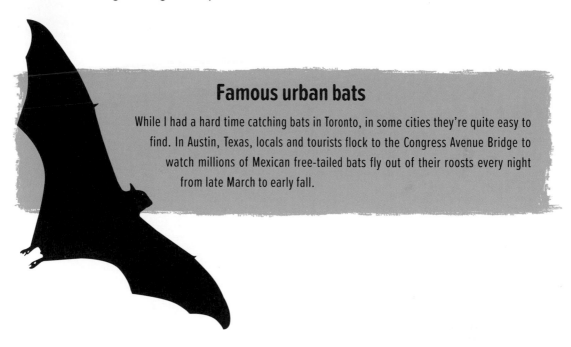

Famous urban bats

While I had a hard time catching bats in Toronto, in some cities they're quite easy to find. In Austin, Texas, locals and tourists flock to the Congress Avenue Bridge to watch millions of Mexican free-tailed bats fly out of their roosts every night from late March to early fall.

URBAN ECOLOGY CHALLENGE

Before I started my research in High Park, I had never seen a bat in the city. They were always there; I just didn't know where or how to look for them. Because bats are nocturnal (they come out to feed at night), they can be hard for us to see. I was so excited to identify my first ones flying in High Park. And I'm still just as excited every time I spot one! I want you to see if you can find some, too.

Try to find a pond or small lake near you. Head out with an adult close to sunset to watch—and don't forget your notebook and headlamp or flashlight! Do you see anything fluttering over the water? You're likely to see some birds (like swallows) grabbing a quick snack before they head to bed, but if you're lucky, you may see some bats, too. If you spot an animal flying erratically (changing direction often), that could be a bat! And you can look for their erratic flight anywhere in your neighborhood. If you do see some bats, write down what time you first noticed them, how many you could count, and how long they stuck around.

If you want help finding bats, check to see if any of the parks or nature centers near you offer evening bat walks.

CHAPTER 2
RATMOBILE TO THE RESCUE

How do animals in cities affect human health?

WHEN MOST PEOPLE PUT OUT RAT TRAPS, it's because they want to get rid of pests. But when Kaylee Byers puts out rat traps, it's so she can collect data and then release the rats right back where she found them. Rats sometimes carry bacteria, viruses, and other germs—called pathogens—that make people sick. Kaylee studies how rats move in cities to understand how these pathogens spread between rats and where rats may share these germs with humans.

WHERE'S THAT RAT?

Kaylee navigated her white panel van—known as the Ratmobile—into an alleyway. In the back, piles of metal traps and lab equipment rattled as the van rolled to a stop. Resting her head against the steering wheel, Kaylee decided that she was officially fed up with Harold.

The trouble had started two weeks ago. Like today, Kaylee had parked her van in an alley in Vancouver's Downtown Eastside, watching the Pacific Ocean peek through the mid-sized industrial and apartment buildings. Kaylee was checking on rat traps she'd set throughout the neighborhood. Baited with peanut butter and oats, these traps had been sitting out all night, and Kaylee was excited to see what she might find in them.

Kaylee hopped out of the Ratmobile and saw her silver rat trap tucked behind a dumpster. As she approached, she heard squeaking and tiny claws scratching frantically against the trap's aluminum sides. With a gloved hand, Kaylee picked up her rat trap and held it at eye level. Inside, two little black eyes peered back at her. She had done it! Kaylee Byers had caught her very first rat.

Kaylee handed the trap to her field partner, Mike Lee, then they climbed into the Ratmobile, closing its doors behind them.

"What should we call this one?" Mike asked as Kaylee pulled on a set of heavy leather gloves.

Kaylee paused. "What about Harold?"

Mike smiled and nodded as they began setting up their equipment.

Before they could collect pathogen data from Harold, they needed to transfer him from the big metal trap to a plastic container with holes poked in the sides. From there Kaylee would be able to anesthetize Harold, or put him to sleep, so she could weigh, measure, and tag him.

TOOLS OF THE TRADE

Kaylee's Ratmobile contains everything she needs to process all the animals she catches, including: scales for weighing, measuring tapes for checking body length, a sleeping gas to anesthetize her animals, tools to take skin samples for DNA, needles to gather blood, and pliers to attach unique metal bands to each rat's ear (so she could tell them apart later).

"You ready?" Kaylee asked Mike. She was standing by with the open container. He nodded and opened the top of the metal trap. As soon as Mike's gloved hand went in, Harold began squeaking and biting.

After a few minutes, Mike called out, "I've got him!" Everything was going smoothly . . . until Harold stretched out his paws, latched on to the side of the trap, and squeezed himself through a thumb-sized hole near the door. Before Mike or Kaylee could react, Harold had pulled his tail out of Mike's hand and scurried off into the van.

For the next 45 minutes, they searched the Ratmobile, but Harold was nowhere to be found. In the hopes of re-catching him, Kaylee baited the trap and left it in the back of the van that night. Twenty-four hours later, the peanut butter and oats were gone and Harold was still at large. This went on for two weeks.

Kaylee sighed and lifted her head off the steering wheel. She jumped out of the van. Flinging open the Ratmobile's back doors, she expected to see an empty trap for the fourteenth day in a row. But Kaylee was surprised! There, licking the last of the peanut butter and oats from the trap floor, was Harold. It seemed that after two weeks of living in the Ratmobile, Harold, just like Kaylee, was fed up and ready to go.

Let's talk about diversity!

Kaylee studies two species of rats in Vancouver—the Norway rat and the black rat. Both species are omnivorous, eating everything and anything (like many people do!). Both originally came from Asia but were moved around the world by humans on our boats.

Rats are part of a group of mammals called rodents. Remember how bats are the second-most species-rich group of mammals? Well, rodents are the first! There are more than 2,400 species of rodents across the globe. Some, like the capybara, are as big as a large dog. Others, like the pygmy jerboa, are tiny (about the length of two quarters side by side).

HOW DO YOU TRACK A RAT?

Getting information on the germs that rats carry is straightforward—unless that rat is like Harold and is hiding in your van. But usually, Kaylee can find out what pathogens a rat has by collecting and testing their blood, saliva, urine, and feces (poop!). But tracking rat movement is much harder. Rats spend a lot of time underground, either in manmade tunnels (like sewers or subways) or in burrows they've dug themselves. Many scientists use Global Positioning System (GPS) tags or collars to provide them with the location of animals as they move through landscapes. However, GPS tags don't work underground, so Kaylee uses DNA to figure out how far her rats are going.

Each one of the cells in your body is filled with DNA. Your DNA is a special set of instructions for making you! And while your DNA is unique to you (unless you have an identical twin), it will be more similar to people that you are closely related to (like your siblings or parents). It's the same with animals like rats.

To look at rat DNA, Kaylee took a small, circular piece of skin from each rat's ear. She sent that skin to a laboratory where other scientists extracted each rat's DNA. Kaylee was then able to see how closely related the rats she was catching in different city blocks were to each other.

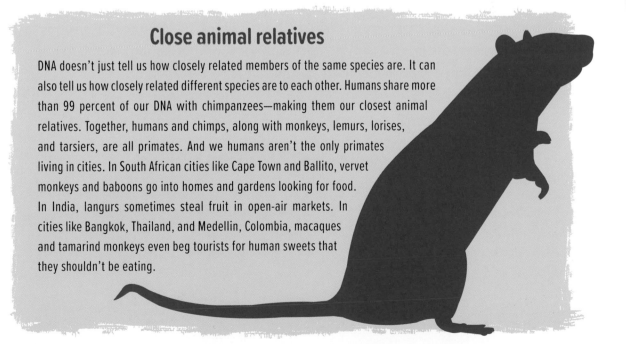

Close animal relatives

DNA doesn't just tell us how closely related members of the same species are. It can also tell us how closely related different species are to each other. Humans share more than 99 percent of our DNA with chimpanzees—making them our closest animal relatives. Together, humans and chimps, along with monkeys, lemurs, lorises, and tarsiers, are all primates. And we humans aren't the only primates living in cities. In South African cities like Cape Town and Ballito, vervet monkeys and baboons go into homes and gardens looking for food. In India, langurs sometimes steal fruit in open-air markets. In cities like Bangkok, Thailand, and Medellin, Colombia, macaques and tamarind monkeys even beg tourists for human sweets that they shouldn't be eating.

Kaylee collected all of these DNA samples (and her pathogen samples) in her Ratmobile! When Kaylee decided she wanted to study urban rats, she knew she would be moving around the city a lot. She also knew that driving her rats to a laboratory would be very stressful for both her and the animals. So, instead of bringing the rats to a lab, Kaylee decided that she would bring her lab to the rats—by building a mobile lab inside a van!

Wait . . . some animals do *better* in cities?

Yep, you read that right—some critters do better in cities! Called urban exploiters, these species often exist in cities at higher population densities (there are more of them around) than in their natural habitats. Sometimes they have adapted to urban living so well that they depend on the resources found in cities to survive. The rats Kaylee studies are an example of urban exploiters, but so are European starlings (a bird species), rock doves (pigeons), and house mice.

HOW FAR DO CITY RATS TRAVEL?

At first, Kaylee thought her rats were moving around the Downtown Eastside neighborhood a lot. But the DNA said otherwise. Kaylee found that rats were most closely related to other rats that lived in the same city block. This means that in cities, rats mostly stay in the city block they were born in.

This is probably because rats don't like to cross roads. Just like rivers or mountains, roads act as a barrier. Many animals can't or won't cross roads because they risk being hit by cars. Animals also don't move if there is a lot of food close to home (just like Harold stayed put in the Ratmobile for his nightly peanut butter and oats!). Think about all the food a rat might find in one city block—dumpsters, garbage cans, and food scraps galore! There's no need for them to roam very far.

This information is helpful to people who want to control rat populations in cities. Because Kaylee's work tells us that rats don't often leave a city block, we can focus on controlling rats block by block, or within single neighborhoods, rather than trying to cover an entire city all at once.

Unexpected guests

Sometimes when scientists trap wildlife, instead of catching the species that they want (the target), they end up with non-target species in their traps. While I have been out catching bats, I've also caught birds in my nets. Kaylee has found skunks, pigeons, and squirrels (which growl!) in her traps.

Cities control rat populations in different ways. Often, they use poisons called rodenticides. Rats, mice, and other rodents eat these poisons and then go back to their burrows and die. However, sometimes these poisons kill other animals, like hawks and owls that eat rats and mice.

Zoo . . . what?

Diseases that jump between animals and humans are called zoonotic diseases, or zoonoses (*zoo-nose-es*). Examples of zoonotic diseases include rabies, Ebola, and influenza. Lots of animals can carry and share zoonotic diseases with humans, so remember—don't touch the wildlife!

In some places, rodenticides don't work because rodents have evolved resistance, meaning they no longer get sick and die from eating these poisons. Instead of poisons, cities can focus on using environmental control. By getting rid of things that encourage the growth of rat populations—like overflowing or open garbage cans—we can make areas in cities less appealing to rats.

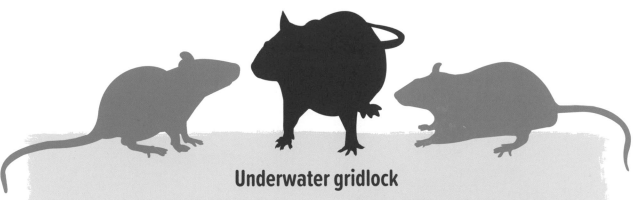

Underwater gridlock

Traffic isn't just a problem for mammals that live on land. Just like rats are at risk of getting hit by cars on roads, whales and dolphins are at risk of getting hit by boats. Whales also have to deal with all the extra sounds that boat traffic produces, which may prevent them from communicating properly.

can we live alongside city rats?

We spend a lot of time trying to remove rats from our neighborhoods because we're worried they may share diseases with us. From North and South America to Western Siberia, rats and other species of rodents spread diseases that make people very sick. But some of Kaylee's work in Vancouver is showing that living with rats may also have effects on people's mental well-being.

With the help of a local community center, Kaylee interviewed people from the Downtown Eastside. Many of these people lived in low-income housing that had rats on the premises. Some of these people had been homeless in the past. Everyone Kaylee interviewed told her they worried about themselves, their children, or their pets getting sick from rats. Some even told her that they couldn't sleep at night because they could hear rats running in their walls or on the floor.

Kaylee's interviews show that not only can rats make us sick, but they also have a big impact on the mental health of people in Vancouver. This information can be used to encourage politicians to run programs to remove rats from buildings, so that everyone can live a little better.

But that doesn't mean we should get rid of all city rats! Rats are important sources of food for other animals, they move seeds around in the landscape, and they mix up soil when they create underground burrows—which helps plants get the nutrients they need to grow. Rats and other rodents are part of our city ecosystems. We just need to work hard to keep them out of our homes and keep them in city green spaces, like parks, instead.

Please don't poison!

Do your parents think there might be rats in your house? If so, ask them to consider not using rat poison. It doesn't always work, and it is bad for other animals. Let them know that snap traps work instead. They can also hire people to block off areas where rodents may be coming in and out of your house and figure out what's causing these rats to stick around (like open trash cans, compost, and untended hedges).

URBAN ECOLOGY CHALLENGE

When Kaylee joined The Vancouver Rat Project, she had to learn to think like a rat. Often, urban ecologists need to guess how animals will move around so they can put their traps in spots the animals are likely to travel through. (I think like a bat when I put up my mist nets.) Kaylee wants you to think like a rat and find some good rat habitat!

After checking with an adult, head out to your backyard, local park, city block, or anywhere you can safely pause and look around. Do you see any possible food sources for rats? Rats can eat almost anything, but they don't like to run out in the open to grab food. They will often run to and from their burrows against objects like walls and hedges. What paths or objects might they run along to get to these food sources? What other city animals might also be eating here? If you were going to set a trap like Kaylee to collect data on the rats in your area, where might you put it? Don't forget your trusty field notebook so you can draw a picture of what you see and label it with spots where you might put your trap.

CHAPTER 3
BEES
AND A BUG VACUUM
Why are cities a good place to study the impact of climate change on bees?

YOU MAY HAVE HEARD THE FAMILIAR BUZZ OF BEES in warmer weather as they search for nectar from flowers. Pollinators like bees are essential for helping plants produce fruits, nuts, and seeds. But as our climate changes, it may be harder for pollinators to find flowers at the right time—which is why Charlotte de Keyzer is on a mission to study how climate change impacts bees and the plants they pollinate.

Charlotte's mission first took her to the Rocky Mountain Biological Laboratory (or RMBL for short), a field station outside Crested Butte, Colorado. RMBL is about the farthest thing from a city you can get. While Charlotte loved working in this undisturbed habitat, she found that it wasn't the best place to answer her questions. Charlotte didn't have the right tools or enough people who could help. Luckily, she knew of a habitat that had plenty of bees *and* people: cities! So, she moved to Toronto, Canada, for phase two of her mission. But urban bee-seeking had its own set of challenges . . .

WHY STUDY BEES IN THE CITY?

Charlotte stood carefully balanced on a step ladder. In her outstretched arms she held a neon-yellow-and-blue vane trap. Charlotte was trying to hang the trap from the branch of an eastern redbud tree, but no matter how far she stretched, she just couldn't get the trap hooked on a branch. Frustrated, Charlotte got off the ladder and sat down.

As she rested under the redbud tree, Charlotte's senses were overwhelmed by the city. Blaring horns from exasperated drivers. The ding of a bicycle passing a group of laughing teenagers. The smell of car exhaust. Charlotte closed her eyes and took a deep breath. Instantly, her nose was filled with the sweet smell of the redbud's flowers. It was so fresh that the rest of the city faded away and was replaced by the memory of crisp mountain air.

Sometimes, Charlotte missed the peace and quiet of the Rockies, where she and a handful of other scientists were the only people around for miles. Scrambling from boulder to boulder up the scree slopes of giant peaks had

Let's talk about diversity!

Worldwide, there are over 20,000 different species of bees! Five thousand of those species live in North America. While most North Americans are familiar with honeybees, these bees are not native to the continent. They are originally from Europe.

In Toronto, there are more than 360 species of native bees. Some, like the Virginia carpenter bee, can grow to the size of a quarter and make their nests in soft wood (you can hear them digging if you listen close enough!). Others, like sweat bees, are bright green and tiny. And some, like the common eastern plasterer bee, which often appears first in the spring, dig their nests in the ground.

always made Charlotte feel like a trailblazing adventurer. But working in the wilderness had its downsides. There were many times when she had lost her balance or slipped. Once, she had almost fallen off a cliff! Had it not been for another ecologist grabbing her backpack, she might not have lived to talk about it.

Charlotte opened her eyes. Thinking about her near-death experience in the Rockies was always a good way to remind herself of what she loved about working in the city. Re-energized, she stood back up, climbed to the top of her ladder, and with a single motion, hooked her vane trap onto the branch of the tree.

What is pollination?

During pollination, pollen grains are moved from the anther of a flower to the stigma. These pollen grains can be moved by wind or attached to the bodies of animals that come to collect plant pollen and nectar to eat. Once pollinated, plants can make fruits, nuts, and seeds, which can grow into new plants.

TOOLS OF THE TRADE

Charlotte's favorite sampling tool is her bug vac—a mini vacuum designed to gently suck up insects. Charlotte modified her bug vacuum by adding a longer tube to make it easier to suck up bees feeding on tree flowers. Once she's caught a bee, she identifies it on the spot and then lets it go!

HOW CAN A VACUUM HELP WITH BEE SCIENCE?

Checking her watch, Charlotte realized that she had just enough time left to test her bug vac—another handy tool she didn't have with her in the Rockies. She got off her ladder and grabbed a handheld contraption that looked like a leaf blower. Surveying the tree, she spotted her target—a slow-moving bee buzzing around a cluster of flowers just below her vane trap.

Charlotte pointed the contraption at the bee and flicked the switch. With a quick *zoosh*, the bug vacuum sucked up the little bee, trapping it in a clear sampling container. As she unscrewed the container from the bug vac, Charlotte turned around to find herself facing a little girl and her father. The pair had been watching her.

"What are you doing?" the girl asked. Charlotte explained that she was using her trusty bug vac to find out what types of bees were visiting the tree. Charlotte held out the sampling container to show the girl the small, metallic-green bee buzzing away inside. "This is a green sweat bee," Charlotte said, "and it just happens to be Toronto's official bee species!"

TOOLS OF THE TRADE

Another way Charlotte catches bees is by hanging brightly colored vane traps from tree branches. Bees are attracted to these traps and fly into a collection container that they can't get out of. Every four days, Charlotte collects these containers and identifies the bees she's caught.

Vane traps are a destructive type of sampling, meaning the bees Charlotte catches die in the process. Ecologists try to use destructive methods as little as possible, but sometimes these methods are the only way to answer our questions. Many scientists who study insects—like Charlotte—have to bring their samples back to a lab so they can identify species using powerful microscopes or by looking at their DNA. Destructive sampling is also how we've built museum collections, which contain plants and animals from all over the world. These collections provide scientists with important details about the types of species that lived in certain areas in the past. This historic information helps us understand how populations have changed over time and continue to change in the present.

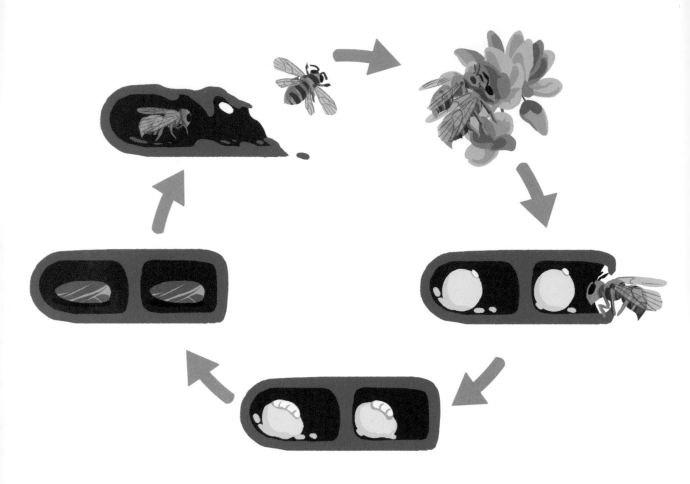

The life cycle of native bees

When you think of bees, you might imagine large colonies living in huge hives. But most native North American bees are actually solitary. Many of these bees build nests by digging holes in the ground. Others nest in cavities that they find in wood, brick mortar, dried-out plant stems, or other hollow structures.

In the spring, adult solitary bees will mate and find (or dig) a cavity to nest in. Then they go out and collect pollen and nectar, which they turn into a ball when they get back to their nest. On top of that ball they lay an egg. These bees will then build a wall that separates this egg and pollen ball from the rest of the nest. This tiny room is called a brood cell. The parent bee will then repeat this process, creating several brood cells in their nest. When the eggs hatch, the bee larvae eat the balls of pollen and nectar. As winter approaches, all the bees in the nest slow down their metabolisms and spend the winter as larvae or adults. In the spring, they chew their way out of the nest and start the cycle again.

HOW CAN EVERYDAY PEOPLE HELP SCIENTISTS UNDERSTAND FLOWERING TIME?

Working in the city has meant that Charlotte gets to share her passion for bees with other people. And she has been able to recruit city residents to help her with her mission.

Charlotte wanted to understand how temperature might be affecting eastern redbud flowering time across the city of Toronto. However, like in the Rocky Mountains, Charlotte would have needed to cover huge distances every day to track this herself. So, to collect all the data she needed, Charlotte created a citizen science program called the Urban Redbud Project.

As part of the program, people living in Toronto tracked the flowering time of redbuds on their properties. People marked the date of flowering for their trees on a calendar and then mailed those calendars to Charlotte. She ended up with data for more than 100 trees across the city. Charlotte also put temperature data loggers in each of these trees and sampled the species of bees visiting them at different times throughout the spring and summer.

How do scientists get people to help?

Charlotte and many urban ecologists need the help of their local communities to make their science possible. But getting that help can be hard. When she first started her project, Charlotte spent a lot of time knocking on doors and dropping off letters asking people to track the redbuds on their properties. Most people weren't interested in helping or didn't want to talk to her. So, Charlotte had to come up with a new plan. She started emailing and calling local gardening, naturalist, and conservation groups instead. Because these people were already interested in city plants, they were much more excited about helping her track redbud flowering time. In the end, Charlotte recruited about 100 people to help her collect data.

HOW DOES FLOWERING TIME CHANGE IN CITIES? WHY DOES THIS MATTER FOR OTHER SPECIES?

While it may not seem like a city has a lot in common with the Rocky Mountains, both landscapes are very complex. A mountain or a city can differ a lot depending on where you are and what time of year it is. For example, in the Rockies, flowers on the same mountain may bloom at different times because of changes in elevation, but also depending on what side of the mountain those flowers are on. In cities, flowers planted close to hot pavement instead of in the shadow of a building may also flower differently.

Variation in biological processes like flowering time impacts how species interact with one another. Species in ecosystems form connected communities, and these species depend on interactions with each other for survival. Charlotte studies the interactions between plants and the insects that visit them. A lot of plants depend on insects, birds, and small mammals for pollination and seed dispersal. In return, these animals rely on plants for nectar, pollen, and fruit to eat.

For plants and pollinators to interact, flowers have to be open at the same time pollinators are around. However, because of climate change, there have been changes to when plants flower and when pollinators arrive—leading to mismatches. Charlotte works to understand these mismatches in cities by studying eastern redbud trees and bees.

What you can do to help native bees

Starting a honeybee hive won't do much to help native bees. In fact, these honeybees eat nectar that native bees depend on, and they can share diseases with them. Instead of a beehive, consider planting native plants that can provide local bee species with pollen and nectar. Try to find plants that flower throughout the spring and summer so food is always available to local bees. Different flowers blooming throughout the spring and summer will help feed a diverse bee community. You can also consider planting a flowering tree, which can support a large number of pollinators!

BUT WHAT DOES ALL THIS MEAN FOR THE BEES?

Although Charlotte hasn't finished this project yet (she's collecting data over several years), she has some early results to share. One of her most surprising results is that the flowering time of redbud trees differs a lot across Toronto. Some trees flower in early spring, while others don't get their flowers until weeks later. These differences in flowering time are caused by differences in temperature across the city. Some places with lots of concrete, like the downtown core, are very hot—even in the shade (you'll learn about why when you meet Carly Ziter on page 81). Trees here tend to bloom earlier in the season. But in larger city parks and close to Lake Ontario, where things are cooler, trees bloom more slowly.

These differences in flowering time mean that there are flowers available to bees for more of the spring. Because of this, Charlotte found that the community of bees visiting the redbud trees throughout the spring was more diverse (there were more bee species) than if the trees had flowered all at once. This is because not all bee species emerge from their winter nests at the same time. Species that spend the winter as adults come out of their nests as soon as temperatures warm up. Other species spend the winter as larvae and develop into adults in the spring before they start looking for food. So, the later a tree blooms in the spring, the more bee species will be around to visit its flowers.

But it isn't all good news for city bees. While changes in temperature may mean a favorite food is available for longer, heat can also affect bees directly. Research from other cities tells us that some species of bees can't survive in cities because they get too hot. Scientists have more work to do to understand how plants and pollinators may be affected by city living. Charlotte is excited to see what future years of her data may tell us.

Is that a bee or a wasp?

It's easy to get wasps and bees confused when they're buzzing around you, but these two insects are quite different. Bees feed on pollen and nectar for their entire life cycle. Wasps mostly feed on nectar as adults, but their young are carnivorous, often eating flies, caterpillars, crickets, and beetle larvae (which means they help control pests that may be feeding on gardens and crops).

Bee or wasp—if a critter is buzzing around you, don't swat! These insects are important parts of our ecosystems. Stay calm, and if possible, move out of that insect's way and it should leave you alone.

URBAN ECOLOGY CHALLENGE

Bees aren't the only pollinators that call cities home. Charlotte thinks you might be surprised by how many different types of pollinators visit the flowers in your neighborhood!

Find a garden somewhere. Take a look at the flowers. What kind of insects do you see visiting them? Can you snap a picture of one? You can use this picture to try and figure out what species it is using books or the internet.

For a bigger challenge, visit the garden every other week for a few months in the summer. Do you notice different types of flowers appearing at different times? Can you learn their names? Can you spot any different pollinators? Try recording some of your observations on a calendar or in your field notebook so you can see how plant and pollinator diversity changes over the spring and summer.

CHAPTER 4
BACKYARD BEAR BUFFET

What happens when humans and wildlife in cities don't get along?

HAVE YOU EVER HAD TO CLEAN UP THE MESS left by a raccoon or other animal rummaging through your family's garbage? It isn't fun. But could you imagine waking up to find a bear tipping over your trash? Not only not fun, but also dangerous. People in cities like Greater Sudbury have always had to deal with backyard bears. But Sudbury residents were worried that more bears were starting to come into the city because the government had canceled the spring bear hunt. They thought that bear populations had grown so much that there wasn't enough natural food to go around. But Jesse Popp wasn't so sure. So, she set out to get to the bottom of this mystery.

Where in the world?

Home to about 165,000 people, Greater Sudbury is Northern Ontario's largest city. Sudbury is known locally as the city of lakes, with more freshwater lakes than any other municipality in Canada—330, in fact!

WHAT'S HIDING IN THE SHED?

"There's an animal in the shed."

Jesse Popp looked up from her book. Her husband, Mike, had his back pressed against their front door as if something was about to break in.

"What kind of animal, Dad?" five-year-old Shyla asked.

"I don't know!" Mike was breathing heavily.

Jesse rushed to the door, handed their two-year-old, Hunter, to Mike, and grabbed her coat. "I'll go take a look."

Outside, gusts of wind rattled the blue tarp shed that covered their driveway. It had been a long, cold winter, and that night, the temperature had dropped to minus 35 degrees Celsius (minus 31 degrees Fahrenheit) with the windchill. Jesse entered slowly, looking behind boxes and under the car. As she moved to the back, she saw it. Tucked in the corner behind their four-wheeler was . . . not a bear, but a coyote.

Jesse inched closer to the animal to get a better look. It raised its head. Jesse could see that it was thin and missing a lot of fur. The coyote stared at Jesse for a moment and then put its head back down and curled up tighter as the wind howled outside.

"Mommy, what was it?" Shyla asked when Jesse stepped back into the house. Hunter clapped in excitement.

"It's a coyote," Jesse said. "But it looks very sick. In the morning we'll call the wildlife center to come and get it. But tonight, we'll just try to make it a bit more comfortable."

Back in the shed, Jesse set down a bowl of warm water and laid out a blanket. She then backed away slowly to join her family inside. With the shed light on, everyone watched quietly. The coyote raised its head, stood up, and curled up on the blanket. With that, Jesse turned off the light and she and her family went to bed.

In the morning, one of Sudbury's wildlife rescue centers picked up the coyote. The vet confirmed that the coyote was sick with a bad case of mange (a skin infection) and would need to spend the rest of the winter at the center getting better.

Five months later, Jesse stood with her family, watching as a wildlife rescue officer positioned a large dog crate at the edge of their backyard, facing the forest.

The wildlife officer slowly lifted the front gate of the dog crate. Out bolted the same coyote the family had met that winter, except now it had a full coat of fur. The coyote took off into the forest as Shyla cheered and Hunter clapped.

"Did you see that?" Shyla asked. "It was so fast! And so big!"

Jesse smiled. "Yes," she said, "it did look much healthier. See, plants and animals, like people, sometimes just need a little help."

Found wildlife that needs help? Call an expert!

Since Jesse is a trained wildlife biologist, she knew what to do when she found the sick coyote in her shed. If you think you've found a sick, injured, or abandoned animal, first get an adult to help. Remember, sick animals can share diseases with humans, and distressed animals may attack if threatened. It's best to leave the animal in its natural setting, as it may not actually need help—and if it does, the next steps will depend on the type of animal you've found. If you're not sure what to do, keep an eye on the animal in trouble (at a safe distance) and call your local wildlife rehabilitation center for advice. They may even have a website that helps you figure out what needs to be done.

ARE "PROBLEM" WILDLIFE REALLY THE PROBLEM?

Though Jesse was in Greater Sudbury to study black bears, not coyotes, she approaches all her research questions in the same way she approached the coyote in her shed—with an understanding that all species on this planet are connected.

Jesse is a member of the Wiikwemkoong Unceded Territory, located on Manitoulin Island in Ontario. She combines the knowledge and teaching of Indigenous communities like her own with the scientific training she received at university and while working with other ecologists. Jesse knows that we need as many perspectives as possible to protect our planet's biodiversity, and she believes it is our job as humans to respect and help other species when we can. Her research finds ways for humans to live together with wildlife, both in and outside of cities. Around the time she and her family found the coyote, Jesse and a team of scientists were working to figure out why American black bears and people were having such a hard time living together.

Human-wildlife conflict

Human-wildlife conflict is any negative interaction between people and animals. Animals tipping over trash cans is only one example. In rural parts of Africa and Asia, elephants may raid farmers' crops. Around the world, predators like lions, cougars, and wolves occasionally eat livestock. In Grand Canyon National Park in the United States, tourists who get too close to elk to try and touch them sometimes get knocked over, leading to injury. Oh, and bears don't just come looking for food in urban areas. They will also head into campsites in search of something to eat. So, make sure to pack away those s'mores!

In the years leading up to Jesse's study, more and more bears had been wandering into Sudbury in search of food. Black bears are omnivores (meaning they eat plants and meat), but they mostly spend their time foraging for berries, plants, and seeds in the wild. When they come into cities, they turn over trash cans looking for leftovers and eat the seeds off the ground around bird feeders. Eating trash is bad for bears, and bears can become dangerous and attack when scared or threatened by people—which is bad for humans.

Jesse and her collaborators knew that if they wanted to help reduce the conflict between bears and humans, they needed to figure out what might be causing them to look for food in the city instead of their natural habitat. The people of Sudbury thought that because the government had canceled the spring bear hunt, the bear population had grown. They thought there wasn't enough natural food for all these new bears, and that hunger was driving them into the city. While this was a possibility, Jesse thought the opposite could also be true. Maybe the bear population wasn't changing at all, but perhaps there was less food available in the wild.

In the summer and fall, bears depend on berries and seeds to gain the weight needed for hibernation. But the amount of berries and seeds available for black bears to eat can change from year to year. In some years, conditions are perfect and berry crops are large. But in other years, because of drought, late frost, severe storms, or fires, plants might not do so well, meaning less berries for bears.

Hibernation

When the weather gets cold and there is less food available, many animals become inactive to save energy. They reduce their body temperature, heartbeat, and breathing, in a safe location like a burrow, den, or cave. Although bears do spend the winter months in dens, they are not true hibernators. They use torpor (like bats) to save energy. One big difference between hibernation and torpor is that animals in torpor can wake up quickly to avoid danger. Female bears actually wake up partway through the winter to give birth!

In hot climates or places with water shortages, some animals do something similar to hibernation called aestivation. Just like you might head to the basement to cool off in the summer, creatures like crocodiles and some tortoises burrow underground to beat the heat.

TOO Many BeaRS OR NOT eNOUGH FOOD?

So, what was causing these bears to wander into Sudbury backyards—more bears sharing the same amount of food, or the same number of bears sharing less food? To figure this out, Jesse looked at data that had been collected in the five years leading up to the cancellation of the spring bear hunt, and the five years after. This information was collected by Ontario's Ministry of Natural Resources and Forestry (MNRF). The MNRF monitors wildlife and plant

populations for a lot of different species, so they had estimates for the amount of seeds and berries that were available for bears to eat in their natural habitat in different years.

The MNRF also relocates "problem" animals that keep wandering into areas with people. Every time a Sudbury resident called about a bear that had shown up at their house multiple times, rangers from the MNRF would livetrap the bear and release it far away from the city. This meant Jesse also had information on the number of bear relocations that had happened in Sudbury over the 10-year period she was interested in.

Jesse used this information to make several comparisons. She looked to see if problem bear captures had gone up in those 10 years. She also compared the number of bear captures in the city to the amount of food bears had access to in their natural habitat.

TOOLS OF THE TRADE

To analyze the data on problem bear captures and food availability, Jesse used an important tool that many scientists rely on . . . a computer! Computers are powerful machines that do everything from running video games to controlling the flow of traffic in cities. Urban ecologists rely on computers for many parts of their work, like storing the data they collect in the field, writing papers, and sharing their science around the world. Many urban ecologists write code in languages like R and Python to perform complex mathematical analyses. The analyses, like the ones Jesse and her collaborators ran, help scientists understand important patterns in their data.

What Jesse found was a little different from what people living in Sudbury thought. While problem bear activity did increase a little bit after the spring bear hunt was canceled, that activity was more strongly related to the amount of natural food available to bears in different years. Jesse found that when bears had low numbers of fruits and seeds available to them in one year, they were more likely to travel farther in search of food when they came out of hibernation—often wandering into places like people's backyards!

HOW CAN WE PREVENT PROBLEM ENCOUNTERS WITH WILDLIFE?

Because of Jesse and her team's work, we know that if there are bad food years, bears will go farther to find something to eat. If bears learn that they can find food where people live, they will continue to come back again and again—sometimes even after they've been captured and moved to another location.

This means that people living in areas with bears need to work hard to make sure their homes don't seem like a bear buffet. They can discourage hungry bears by keeping trash in bear-proof areas or structures, not leaving pet food outside, and by packing up bird feeders when bears come out of hibernation in the spring. By minimizing the amount of food we leave out, we can teach bears that cities aren't good places to find their next meal.

But this doesn't just apply to bears and food. We share our cities with many different types of animals. And while seeing these animals might be fun and interesting, we should discourage them from coming close to humans and our pets. Bears aren't the only animal that can attack when scared or threatened. Other wildlife, like the coyote in Jesse's shed, might do the same—especially if they're hurt. However, if we work toward making our homes unappealing to animals and give them lots of space when we see them outside, we should be able to peacefully coexist. We need everyone to do what they can to help conserve nature.

Roads and railways—oh my!

Roads are a dangerous barrier that many wildlife try to cross. Some animals die in the process. Sometimes, both people and animals get hurt, like when a car collides with a moose.

We've spent a lot of time studying and trying to prevent these dangerous roadway collisions. But Jesse is interested in what happens around railways. Just like roads, railways are a danger for animals trying to cross, but we don't know how these railways are impacting wildlife. What kind of species die in railway collisions? Are there hotspots where wildlife are more likely to get hit? How can we stop these collisions from happening? These are just some of the questions Jesse is focused on answering.

URBAN ECOLOGY CHALLENGE

Sometimes animals leave behind clues that let people and other animals know they've been around. When Jesse was very young, she learned how to identify these animals without actually seeing them. This is something she's been teaching Shyla and Hunter to do, too. Jesse wants to challenge you to find some of these clues in your own neighborhood.

When animals walk through snow, soil, or mud, their feet leave behind tracks. Go online and look up tracks for some local critters. Draw some of these tracks in your notebook and see if you can find any of them outside (after checking with an adult first). With a little time and practice, you should be able to recognize the tracks of all these animals when you see them!

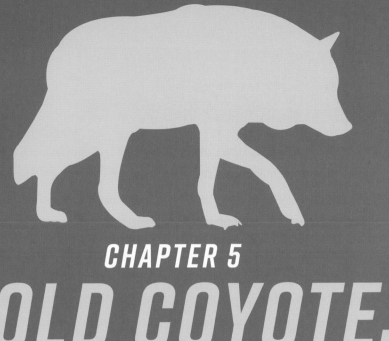

CHAPTER 5

BOLD COYOTE, BASHFUL COYOTE

How are humans changing animal behavior in cities?

SOME ANIMALS DON'T SEEM TO HAVE A PROBLEM getting close to humans. Maybe you've had a squirrel try to steal your snack, or a pigeon follow you around. But not all animals are this bold. Just like humans, individual animals of the same species respond to situations differently. These differences in behavior are called personality. Yes, animals have personalities, too! Some animals may be shy and avoid taking risks. Other animals may be bold and act unafraid in new situations. These differences in personality shape how individual animals interact with each other, but also with people (like you) in cities. Chris Schell studies the personalities of city coyotes. He wants to understand how the things we humans do are changing the way coyotes act around us.

HOW many COPS DOES IT Take To wake UP a COYOTE?

By Chris's estimates, he had just under an hour before the coyote lying on the picnic table in front of him woke up. And that was the best-case scenario. The coyote was in a light sleep. Despite the drugs they'd given it, the animal could be woken up at any time by a loud enough noise.

Chris was standing with his mentor, Dr. Stewart Breck, and a few other ecologists at the edge of a baseball field. The field, still partially lit by large outdoor lights, had long been empty. Chris checked his watch. It was two o'clock in the morning. Out of the corner of his eye, Chris thought he saw a white car slow down as it drove by. But he didn't pay too much attention. He and his team had a coyote to process. Fast.

Working quickly, Chris and Stewart began to pull items out of their processing bags. As Chris lined up tools and sample collection jars, he thought he saw a white car drive by again. *Was that the same car I just saw?* Chris wondered. He paused for a moment, then decided he must be seeing things.

"Let's get started with the easy stuff," Chris said.

Stewart pulled out a clipboard and pen. "I'm ready when you are, Chris."

Together, the two recorded the coyote's key physical details—length, weight, sex, and overall body condition. Next, Chris took clippings of fur from the animal's body and placed them into collection containers. The two worked quickly and quietly while the coyote slumbered.

Where in the world?

Chris currently works in Tacoma, Washington, a coastal city that is home to around 210,000 people. Chris has also worked with coyotes in Denver, Colorado, and at the National Wildlife Research Center's Predator Research Facility in Millville, Utah.

"Time for blood?" Stewart asked.

"Yes," Chris replied, "let's get this done, wake this animal up, and head home!"

As they prepared syringes and tubes to collect blood from the coyote, Chris glanced up. *Are my eyes playing tricks on me?* he thought. Sitting on the road in front of them was the same car Chris was now sure he had seen drive by twice. Chris squinted. The lights from the baseball field were just bright enough for him to make out a blue logo on the side of the car.

"Hey, did you notice—" Chris began. But before he could finish, he was being blinded by headlights.

Chris panicked briefly. He looked away from the police cruiser's headlights and down at the coyote. Had its eyelid just fluttered?

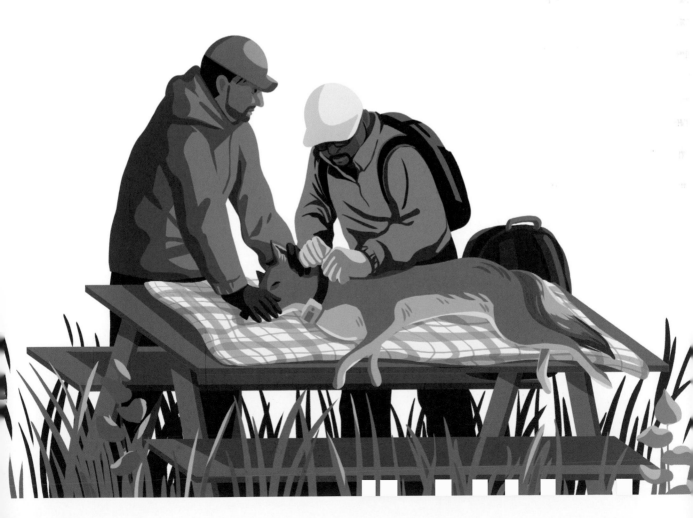

"We need to get this animal processed *now*," Chris said firmly. He picked up a syringe and pulled the cap off the needle. As he did, he heard a car door slam.

Chris's hands began shaking. Worried the coyote would wake up, he handed the needle to Stewart and placed both hands on the animal in case it started moving. Stewart swiftly put the syringe into a blood vessel on the coyote's leg.

One of the other ecologists bounded off toward the approaching police officer. Chris overheard a whispered conversation as the coyote's blood filled the sample vials. Chris and Stewart completed the sampling, wiped down the coyote's leg, and had the blood packed away in no time. No sooner had they finished than the person talking with the police came back up to the bench.

"I've explained and everything is fine, but the cops are wondering if they can watch us put a GPS collar on this coyote."

Chris smiled. The coyote was still snoozing gently.

"Sure," he said. "Just tell them that we'll need them to stay quiet."

TOOLS OF THE TRADE

Chris uses two methods to sample coyotes in the wild. Sometimes he needs to livetrap coyotes to collect information and put GPS collars on them.

Because livetrapping can be stressful for animals, Chris also uses camera traps. Camera traps don't actually "trap" an animal but simply take its picture. Chris sets his camera traps up on trees, buildings, or other structures. When an animal walks by, its movement triggers the camera. Chris then downloads the data from the memory cards of the traps and identifies the animals from the photos.

WHAT DO COYOTE PERSONALITIES HAVE TO DO WITH HUMANS?

Chris had a good reason for collecting data from that coyote in the baseball field. He cares a lot about the animals he works with because they have a bad reputation (like bats!). Coyotes are an apex predator, meaning they are at the top of their food chain—no other animals eat them. As the top predator, coyotes help to keep entire ecosystems healthy by controlling the populations of other species like rabbits, small deer, and rodents. But many city residents don't like having coyotes around. Though coyotes often avoid humans, sometimes they wander too close to people's homes in search of food. They may even eat small pets that are left outside unattended. Chris wants to find out whether some coyotes have developed these bolder behaviors as a result of living alongside humans, or if this is just part of the natural differences in animal personality.

Rowdy 'roos

Coyotes aren't the only animals whose behavior can change when they get close to humans. Charles-Alexandre Plaisir studies the survival of baby eastern gray kangaroos in Wilsons Promontory National Park, Australia. While the populations Charlie works with are wild, some individuals are getting a little too used to the tourists flocking to see them in their natural habitats. This hasn't created problems for the kangaroos Charlie studies, yet, but on the outskirts of cities like Canberra, kangaroos and people regularly get into conflict. Kangaroos graze on people's lawns, come up to them looking for food, or have dangerous interactions with pet dogs—sometimes leading to injuries. Whether in natural landscapes or cities, giving wildlife lots of space is safer and healthier for everyone.

HOW CAN WE STUDY COYOTE PERSONALITY?

Chris uses several methods to study coyote personality. Sometimes he livetraps them—like he did that night in the baseball field—so he can fit them with GPS collars to see where they move in the city. Livetrapping coyotes also lets him collect data on the animals' health and DNA (like Kaylee collected from her rats) to see if personality traits are shared between close relatives.

But studying coyotes in the wild can be hard. They are elusive and difficult to capture. So, to study long-term changes in animal behavior, Chris worked with a captive group of coyotes at a research station in Utah. He wanted to see if coyotes exposed to humans on a regular basis would change their behavior over time. Chris also wanted to test if parent coyotes would teach their puppies these same behaviors.

Over several years, Chris observed eight pairs of breeding coyotes and two litters of their puppies. To figure out how bold or shy individual animals were, Chris used a foraging test. Normally, caregivers at the research station would scatter coyote food throughout the enclosures, and the coyotes would come out to feed after the caregivers had left. Instead, Chris asked the caregivers to place the coyotes' food in three piles close to the front of their enclosures. He then sat in front of these piles of food (on the other side of the fence!) and recorded which puppies and adults came out of hiding to eat. Chris repeated this test several times a week for 10 weeks.

With the first litter of puppies, Chris found that shy parents tended to give birth to shy puppies who were less likely to feed at piles of food placed in front of people. Bold parents tended to have bold puppies who were willing to take a risk and feed in front of Chris while he watched. But this changed! The second year that Chris went back to watch the coyotes, all of the shy parents from the first year had become bolder. And all the new puppies were willing to feed in front of people faster and more often.

Chris's experiment with captive coyotes tells us important things about how coyotes in the wild behave. His data suggests that when coyotes are frequently exposed to people, they are willing to take greater risks. And they pass these bold behaviors on to their puppies. This means that city living may be encouraging these animals to become bolder over time. These bold behaviors might create conflict between people and coyotes (just like with Jesse's bears) because bold coyotes may be more likely to get close to humans.

However, we can discourage boldness in coyotes. If you see a coyote, instead of trying to get closer to it, make some noise and scare it off. If you're out walking your dog, keep it on a leash and away from these animals. And, perhaps most importantly, don't leave your small pets alone outside. Discouraging coyotes from getting close to us and our pets will help humans coexist with them in cities.

Crafty raccoons

Raccoons—affectionately nicknamed trash pandas in many places—are another common, mid-sized mammal species that Chris sees on his camera traps. Raccoons are are crafty animals, known for being good problem solvers. They use their nimble paws to open up trash cans and eat human leftovers.

Chris wants to understand how all the extra food left out in cities is affecting both raccoon and coyote health and behavior.

WHERE DO WE FIND COYOTES IN CITIES?

Chris isn't just interested in how coyotes behave around people. He also wants to understand how they move around cities. But just like Charlotte needed help from Toronto residents to collect data on redbud trees, Chris couldn't do all this tracking on his own. So, he started the Grit City Carnivore Project (GCCP) with Point Defiance Zoo and Aquarium, Northwest Trek Wildlife Park, and Metro Parks Tacoma, all in Tacoma, Washington. The GCCP is a long-term research project that is trying to understand how urban carnivores are dealing with city living. As one part of the GCCP, Chris and his collaborators use camera traps to collect data on where coyotes roam in the city. One of his favorite parts of this project is the number of community members who have called and asked if they can install camera traps at their houses and schools.

Once he knows where coyotes go in the city, Chris wants to figure out how their movement relates to the amount of green space available. But because the camera traps capture images of all kinds of wildlife, the GCCP is also using this data to understand the overall diversity of mammals across Tacoma. One question they're hoping to answer is how mammal diversity may relate to average neighborhood income and historical policies, like redlining, that restricted where certain types of people were allowed to live in cities.

Let's talk about diversity

Coyotes are members of the Canidae family, which comes from the Latin word *canis*, meaning dog. This family of carnivores contains foxes, wolves, jackals, domestic dogs, and raccoon dogs (which aren't closely related to raccoons, even though their faces look similar).

While the GCCP is fairly new, it seems like coyotes and other urban carnivores are mainly found in Tacoma's richest neighborhoods. These affluent areas also tend to have the largest and nicest green spaces in the city. The first results from the GCCP suggest that not everyone in cities has equal access to biodiversity. Remember how we talked about all the benefits nature provides us with? Well, if we don't all have equal access to nature, that means that not everyone gets these benefits. And that's not fair. Data from Chris's project, and others around North America, can be used to encourage urban planners to make sure that all neighborhoods have green spaces capable of supporting equal amounts of biodiversity. And that's good news for animals *and* humans.

Why do richer areas sometimes have bigger parks?

Like the GCCP is discovering in Tacoma, wealthier neighborhoods in many cities often have higher biodiversity. This is called the "luxury effect." Richer neighborhoods generally have larger and better maintained green spaces that can support a greater number of species. Lower-income neighborhoods, which often have large groups of racial and ethnic minorities living in them, do not have the same kind of access to the same amount of nature.

One thing (among many) that played a big role in shaping income inequality in North American cities is redlining. Redlining was the unjust government-sponsored policy of denying services (like banking or getting a home loan) to people living in certain areas. Banks would draw actual red lines around neighborhoods on maps to highlight areas where they would not invest. Redlining was largely used to prevent minorities from buying homes, leading to racially segregated neighborhoods. Because of redlining, these neighborhoods remained less prosperous, as wealth in other—often whiter—neighborhoods grew. Although redlining is now illegal, its effects can still be seen in many urban communities, shaping where we find biodiversity—and who has access to nature—today.

WHAT DOES ALL OF THIS MEAN FOR URBAN COYOTES?

Coyotes are here to stay in cities, so it's our job to learn how to live alongside them. Chris's work on coyote personality shows that coyotes living close to humans get bold, so we need to work to discourage this. The data about coyote movement that he's collecting from camera traps is also important information for managing this species. It tells us where we can find these animals in cities and where conflict might occur. Chris hopes his research can help stop conflict between coyotes and people before it even occurs.

Can you ID these animals' butts?

Camera trapping can be hard. Often the camera catches only a small part of an animal as it's running by. In his work, Chris sees a lot of animal butts. Can you guess what common urban animals these might be by looking at their bottoms?

URBAN ECOLOGY CHALLENGE

In Chris's opinion, watching animals is never boring. He also thinks you're never too young to start studying animal behavior—so he's got an experiment for you to try. Grab your notebook and an adult and head outside. Try to spot a small animal like a pigeon or a squirrel in a local park. Start about 20 big steps away from the animal. Begin walking closer and closer. How many steps can you take toward the animal before it runs or flies away? Write that number down in your notebook.

Behavioral biologists like Chris call this distance the "flight initiation distance" or "flight zone." If a predator or other threat enters an animal's flight zone, the animal will run away. Try it again with a different animal. Does this animal move away after the same number of steps? Does it let you get closer? See if you can find two animals that respond differently to you walking toward them.

CHAPTER 6
MICROPLASTICS, MAJOR PROBLEMS
How does the pollution we create affect city animals?

EVER SPOTTED PESKY PLASTICS while you've been outside enjoying nature? Maybe the straw from a juice box left on the jungle gym? A water bottle rolling around on the sidewalk? An old grocery bag caught on rocks in the river? In cities, pollution in the form of plastic, waste, chemicals, smoke, and other contaminants regularly enters natural systems. This pollution can change and damage ecosystems, so we need to understand what effects it has. Rachel Giles studies how pollution from roadways harms communities of species living in streams and rivers. But unlike the other scientists in this book, Rachel studies critters that are a bit harder to spot with your naked eye. She spends her time sifting tiny invertebrates out of the bottom of streams—all in the middle of the winter. Why? Because these teeny creatures can tell us big things about how our pollution impacts city nature—and us, too.

WHAT'S WAITING IN A FLOODED RIVER?

It was very cold and the day was not going as planned. Rachel Giles and her two field assistants, Anto and Hayley, stood about 6 meters (20 feet) away from the bank of the Humber River in Toronto. At least, that's how far they thought they were from the river. They couldn't actually see the banks—or any ground between them and the river. An unusual warm spell had caused much of the snow in the area to melt, flooding their entire field site.

"What do you think, Rach? Can we still sample?" Hayley asked.

Rachel rubbed her forehead, thinking. She had no way of knowing how deep the water was or if they could even make it to the river safely, but she needed to collect samples from the river water to keep her project on track.

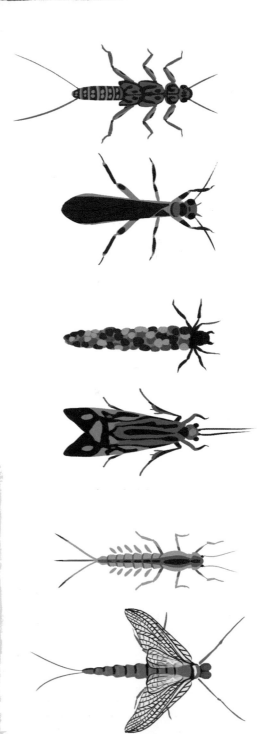

Inverte-what?

Most animals on the planet (about 97 percent) are invertebrates—organisms that do not have a spine or a bony skeleton. They can be so small that you need a microscope to see them, like bacteria, or as large as the giant squid—which can grow to be 13 meters (43 feet) long, or longer than most telephone poles are tall! Spiders, butterflies, starfish, and single-celled amoebas are also invertebrates. On the other hand, humans, fish, mammals, and birds are vertebrates. We have a spinal cord and a bony skeleton to provide our bodies with support.

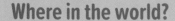

Where in the world?

The Humber River, originally called Cobechenonk (meaning "leave the canoes and go back") by the Anishinaabe, starts on the Niagara Escarpment in Mono, Ontario, Canada, and empties into Lake Ontario. It's about 126 kilometers (78 miles) long. While that may seem big, it's only about 2 percent as long as Africa's Nile River (the longest river in the world).

"Let's try it," Rachel responded.

As Anto set up their field equipment on a nearby footbridge, Hayley and Rachel pulled on their sampling clothes. Although Toronto was in the middle of a winter warm spell, it was by no means warm. The temperature hovered around 2 degrees Celsius (36 degrees Fahrenheit) and they were about to wade into water that was just as cold. Rachel and Hayley had to stay warm and dry to prevent hypothermia—a dangerous condition where the body can't warm itself up. Squeezing into hip waders that went up to her armpits, Rachel wished for a moment that she had chosen a summer field project that involved far less clothing.

Rachel and Hayley waded across the flooded ground while Anto watched from the bridge. As the water got deeper, Rachel held up her hand and Hayley stopped. "Why don't you wait here," Rachel said. "I'll collect the samples and call if I need anything." Hayley nodded as Rachel continued forward on her own.

Water now at her mid-thighs, Rachel suddenly felt the ground become mushy. She had found the riverbank, but the soil was so waterlogged that it was collapsing under her weight and pulling her in. Rachel took a deep breath and slowly tried to turn around. But with every step back up the bank, she sank deeper.

"Rach, are you okay?" Hayley called.

"No!" Rachel yelled back. "I'm sinking!" Quickly scanning the area, Rachel pointed at a tree hanging over the river. "That tree! Meet me there, but don't come any closer to the bank."

Now nearly chest-deep in the river, Rachel shuffled toward Hayley and the tree. Cold water splashed into her waders. "Just a few more steps," she muttered, trying to stop herself from panicking as icy water soaked her shirt. "Just a few more . . ."

Before Rachel could say "steps," Hayley was there, hanging on to the tree, arm outstretched. Rachel grabbed her hand. With a little tug Hayley hoisted Rachel out of the sinking bank. Clinging to the tree, the two quickly collected their samples and walked back to the van.

Anto had packed up the equipment and was waiting for them. "What were you two doing hanging on to that tree?" he asked. Hayley explained how Rachel had gotten stuck.

"Huh. Sounds scary," Anto said, unlocking his phone. "But it kinda looked like you were having fun." He held up the screen and flipped through a few pictures. It really did look like they were actually having a blast hanging off the side of the tree. Staring at the pictures, slightly chilly from the water that had soaked her shirt, all Rachel could do was laugh.

HOW DO WE STUDY POLLUTION IN CITY STREAMS?

While Rachel, Anto, and Hayley could see the danger of that flood right away, Rachel's research focuses on threats that are harder to spot—but just as important to the health of city ecosystems. A lot of stuff gets washed off roads into waterways like the Humber River. This road-runoff contains microplastics from car tires, small pieces of metal, gas, and chemicals from vehicle exhaust. Cities that get snow in the winter also put salt on roads to prevent them from icing over. This road salt washes into streams and rivers, too. While all of this pollution can affect any creatures living in or around these waterways, Rachel looks at the effects of wintertime pollution on invertebrates.

Rachel chose to study the Humber River because it flows through rural, suburban, and urban areas before it empties into Lake Ontario. To understand how pollution and invertebrate communities change across these different parts of the river, Rachel sampled three sites: Toronto (urban), Brampton (suburban), and Albion Hills (rural). She returned to these sites every month from December to May to understand how pollution might change across the season, too.

What are microplastics?

Microplastics are tiny pieces of plastic that are often smaller than your baby fingernail, or less than 5 millimeters (0.2 inches). They can be created when larger plastics break down, but are also shed from synthetic clothing and used in health and beauty products like toothpaste. Microplastics are so small, our water filtration systems can't capture them, so they make their way into our waterways. We are still learning about the effects of microplastics on wildlife, and Rachel and the other scientists in her lab are working hard to figure this out. In the meantime, countries like Canada, France, the United States, New Zealand, and the United Kingdom have banned some kinds of microplastics in certain products.

HOW DOES WINTER POLLUTION AFFECT STREAM ECOSYSTEMS?

At each of her sampling locations, Rachel collected water and sediment (rock and dirt) samples to measure the amount of pollution. She also sampled benthic invertebrates—organisms that live and spend the winter in the sediment of riverbeds. Rachel took her samples back to the laboratory, where she analyzed the chemicals in the sediment and water, separated out the microplastics, and identified using a microscope the types of invertebrates she'd collected.

While Rachel hasn't finished examining all of her data, so far the patterns match what she expected to see. Rachel has found some salt and microplastics at all three sites, but her urban site has a lot more pollution than both the suburban and rural sites. Rachel's data also shows that in the city, the amount of pollution in the water fluctuates a lot more throughout the winter. These big changes may be making it harder for invertebrates to adapt and stay alive in city waterways.

Rachel is also finding that there are fewer species present (the communities are less diverse) at urban sites. The species missing from city communities—animals like stoneflies, caddisflies, and mayflies—are sensitive organisms that cannot deal with the extra pollution in the water. Species like midges and aquatic earthworms, though, are able to stick around even with contamination.

Who else is living in our water?

Fish are another important part of stream ecosystems, but it can be hard to study them without stressing them out. Most scientists study fish by catching them with nets or by using electrofishing (where a small jolt of electricity knocks the fish out temporarily). All this handling is hard on fish, which is why ecologist Rowshyra Castañeda tested if underwater cameras could be used to study them instead. Thanks to her work, we now know that these cameras work well in clear water. Rowshyra has used these cameras to monitor invasive fish species (those added to streams by humans) in the Swartkops River in South Africa and in agricultural ponds in Ceres, South Africa.

TOOLS OF THE TRADE

Rachel samples invertebrate communities using a Hess Sampler. A Hess Sampler looks like a large soup stock pot without a bottom with a long funnel-shaped net connected to the side. To use it, Rachel has to first make sure she can actually get it into the water. Sometimes that means she has to break away ice! Once it's in the water, Rachel sets the Hess Sampler on the bottom of the river, filling it with rocks and sediment. She then puts her hands through the top of the Hess Sampler and wipes the rocks with her hands, peeling off any invertebrates that may be stuck. As she does this, the stream's current carries the loose invertebrates into a collection jar at the end of the funnel-shaped net.

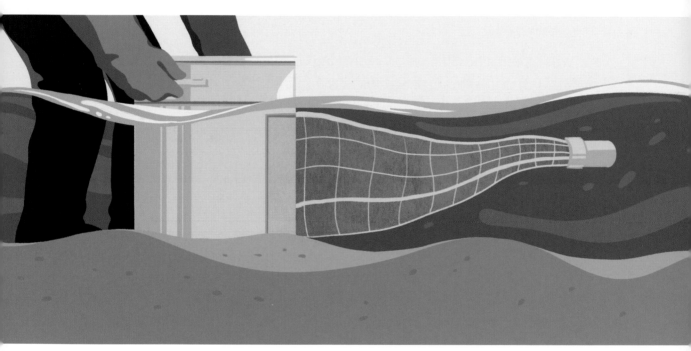

What can we use instead of road salt?

Road salt may be bad for our environment, but it is important for keeping our roads safe during the winter. To reduce the amount of salt needed to keep ice off roads, some cities apply brine solutions (a mixture of salt and water) before big storms. Solid salt often bounces off roads, so brine helps reduce that waste. Some places are also experimenting with using beet juice instead of salt. But just because beet juice is natural doesn't mean it won't affect our waterways. So, we still need to test it!

If you want to reduce the amount of ice that forms around your own home, make sure to shovel your snow. Clearing snow before it gets packed down and turns to ice may mean that you can use less salt on your steps, sidewalks, and driveway.

WHAT CAN INVERTEBRATES TELL US ABOUT THE WHOLE AQUATIC COMMUNITY?

Rachel's results are already showing us that wintertime pollution is having a big effect on the very small species that live in our waterways. While Rachel is only looking at the impacts on invertebrates, these creatures can tell us a lot about the overall health of the entire community. The smallest parts of ecosystems—like invertebrate in streams—are often the most sensitive to change. And because many aquatic invertebrates are food for other stream creatures, when their populations decline, eventually the populations of other species will, too. If invertebrate communities are suffering because of winter pollution, other organisms in urban waterways are also likely being impacted. It just may take longer to see these effects.

Unhealthy streams are bad news for humans, too. Healthy streams and rivers help prevent flooding, filter water, and provide important habitat for many other species that provide ecosystem services. But pollution is something we can change. Rachel hopes her work will motivate cities to come up with ways to prevent salt, microplastics, and other pollutants from entering our waterways, and reduce or even eliminate their use. She also hopes her research will encourage everyday people like you to create less waste in their day-to-day lives.

Where else in the world?

Rachel also studies the effects of plastics in Vietnam's waterways. She works in hot, humid mangroves to understand how much plastic is present in the environment, what effects it has on local species, and how much may be making its way to the ocean. Rachel works closely with a local not-for-profit group that has built a "trash trap" to remove plastics from rivers before they reach the ocean. She is helping this group understand how their device might benefit critters living in the Song Hong or Red River.

URBAN ECOLOGY CHALLENGE

Rachel always has fun searching for tiny critters under rocks and in gravel. So much fun that she wants you to give it a try!

Grab an adult and go find a small creek or stream in your neighborhood. Look around and pick up a rock close to the riverbank. Do you see anything underneath? There should be some invertebrates hiding in the indent the rock left behind, or stuck to the rock's bottom. Put some of the animals you found in an ice cube tray filled with water to help you see them better. Make sure to keep them wet and out of the sun. Try drawing one in your notebook! When you're done, make sure to gently return the invertebrates you've collected to the bottom of the stream. Try looking up your local invertebrates to see if you can identify which ones you found.

Remember—streams and rivers can be dangerous. Sometimes, after big storms, even small streams can flow very fast. Make sure you choose a small stream, bring an adult with you, and go out during the summer when it's warm and hasn't recently rained.

CHAPTER 7
BIRDWATCHING BIAS
What happens when citizen science doesn't tell us the whole story?

THE NEXT TIME YOU'RE OUTSIDE, listen closely. Do you hear anything singing from the trees or rooftops? Chances are you've seen birds in your city before. But how many species visit your neighborhood? How do those species differ from the birds elsewhere in the city? Many urban ecologists want to understand where we find different species of wildlife. And—as you've learned—they sometimes get community help to collect data. Take eBird. Anyone can create a free online account and record when and where they see different birds. Scientists then use this data to answer questions that require lots of information. But scientists like Deja Perkins worry this data may not tell us the whole story. Because eBird volunteers choose when and where they collect data, Deja is concerned that not all areas are being sampled equally— especially in cities. She wants to know if eBird data is actually giving us an accurate picture of urban bird diversity.

WHAT HAPPENS WHEN PEOPLE DON'T WANT SCIENTISTS IN THEIR NEIGHBORHOODS?

"What are you doing here?"

Deja Perkins looked up from her clipboard. A woman she'd smiled at a few moments earlier now stood directly in front of her, and her expression wasn't very friendly.

"I'm a scientist," Deja said, explaining that she had come to observe birds in the neighborhood. The woman looked skeptical, so Deja pulled a flyer off her clipboard and handed it to her. "This is part of a much larger project!" Deja continued excitedly. "We've got everyday people helping us survey birds across Durham, Raleigh, and Chapel Hill. Perhaps you'd be interested in helping us collect data?"

The woman aggressively handed the flyer back. "I need you to leave," she said roughly.

Deja was flustered. Usually, once she explained her work to folks, they were excited and encouraging. This woman was the opposite.

"Pardon?" Deja said.

"I need you to leave," the woman repeated. "You're making me uncomfortable."

Deja nodded. "Of course, I'll just sample somewhere else."

Deja speed-walked away. The whole interaction had put her on edge. She decided she would find another location to sample, perhaps somewhere more public. Not too far from the original spot, Deja found a small pond with a walking trail around it. *Perfect*, she thought.

Sing me a song, birdie

The sounds birds make can be grouped into calls and songs. Songs are complex vocalizations made by birds (often, but not always, male birds) for specific reasons—generally to attract mates or defend territory. Bird songs are also structured, meaning they are made up of repeated notes that you can recognize. But listen closely: many individual birds have a repertoire or different versions of the same song! Unlike songs, calls are less complex, shorter noises made by birds to do things like signal danger or a need for help, or to ask for food.

It was quiet and overcast, and after the unsettling interaction she'd just had, Deja wished there were more people around. Getting ready to begin her sampling, Deja took a 360-degree photo of the site and pulled out her clipboard again. As she scanned the area, Deja caught sight of a small black bird flying from bush to bush in the distance. Excitedly, she grabbed her binoculars, hoping to identify it. But what she saw instead made her heart sink.

"I don't believe this!" Deja said under her breath. Just past the bush was the same woman who had asked Deja to leave. And now she had a dog.

Maybe she's just out walking her dog, Deja thought. *It must be a coincidence.* But deep down, she knew it wasn't. Deja was shook. She thought about canceling the data collection altogether. But she was in a public space. She had the right to be there. So, for the next 10 minutes Deja recorded every bird she saw and heard, determined to not let the woman intimidate her. Before Deja knew it, she had forgotten all about the woman watching her. Instead, she was filled with the joy that bird-watching always gave her.

The woman with the dog did not budge for the entire sampling period. Once she had collected her data, Deja quickly packed everything up and made her way to her car. As she pulled away from the curb, Deja felt a sense of relief. Although she was unnerved, she was glad that she had stood her ground. *At least I saw my first green heron today*, Deja thought happily, as the sun finally peeked through the clouds.

HOW CAN BIAS AFFECT URBAN ECOLOGISTS?

Not all encounters between urban ecologists and the community are fun. Deja may never know exactly why the angry woman refused to read her flyer and wanted her gone, but it probably had to do with the fact that Deja is a Black woman.

For Black scientists like Deja, Chris, and me, doing research in cities and the wilderness can be hard because of people's racial bias. We talked about how bias happens when we favor one group, thing, or location over others. Well, with racial bias, people may make harmful assumptions about others based on the color of their skin. Racial bias means that sometimes people wrongly think Black, Indigenous, and other scientists of color are suspicious. Those people may be more likely to call the police on us. It may also mean that people (including the police) are less likely to believe us when we say we are scientists studying nature in cities.

While racial bias can harm scientists working in the field, scientists' own biases—or bias in our data—can impact our research if we are not careful. In urban ecology, bias may affect where we choose to look for wildlife in a city. This is exactly what Deja is worried about.

TOOLS OF THE TRADE

Deja doesn't just observe birds using binoculars—she also catches and bands them! Deja spent some time working with a team to capture and study red-tailed hawks. She and the team set traps along the highways of Starkville, Mississippi. Once they caught a hawk, they placed a small metal band with a unique number on its leg (kind of like a bracelet) before letting it go. These bands, just like the microchips in my bats, help researchers keep track of individual hawks in the population. This lets them figure out if the population is healthy and growing from year to year.

HOW COULD BIAS AFFECT WHAT WE KNOW ABOUT CITY BIRDS?

If the angry woman had read Deja's flyer, she would have learned that Deja was collecting data for a citizen science project started by scientists in Durham, Raleigh, and Chapel Hill (known as North Carolina's research triangle): the Triangle Bird Count.

Deja and the other scientists she works with are worried about the spatial bias in eBird data. Some areas are very well sampled by volunteers, while other parts of the city have no data at all. Deja is worried that this bias in where data on urban birds is coming from might be caused by who is collecting this data. eBird volunteers may have their own biases that influence where and when they collect data. They may choose to look for birds in their favorite parts of the city or in places where they know birds will be easy to find. Deja is also worried birders may avoid certain areas of cities that have reputations for being "rougher," or that people may stick to observing birds in locations where everyone in the community looks similar to them. Just like Chris with his coyotes, Deja is concerned that this may mean we are learning less about nature (or the lack of it) in low-income neighborhoods and communities where mainly Black, Indigenous, and other people of color live. Deja knows scientists who have answered questions using eBird. She's even contributed observations herself. But while she knows the power of eBird, Deja thinks we need to look at the data more closely to see what might be missing, especially in cities.

Is citizen science the best name?

You may often hear scientific projects that have been started by scientists and involve members of the community being called citizen science. But more and more scientists are opting to call these types of projects community, public, or volunteer science instead. Not all members of our communities may be citizens of the country they currently live in, but everyone is welcome to contribute to scientific discovery.

Let's talk about diversity!

Birds are the only living dinosaurs. Yep, you read that right. The chicken you might sometimes eat for dinner is a dinosaur. Birds evolved from small, feathered theropods. Today, you can find birds all over the globe (including Antarctica) with about 10,000 species worldwide.

The pigeon cannon

Some scientists, like Elizabeth Carlen, study specific species of birds living in cities. Elizabeth studies pigeons in New York City to understand how city living may be affecting their evolution. To do this, Elizabeth has to catch pigeons so that she can take a sample of their DNA and compare it to DNA from other pigeons (just like Kaylee does with her rats). Elizabeth catches pigeons using a pigeon cannon—a tiny handheld device that shoots out a net. It's pretty cool to see in action!

HOW CAN WE CHECK FOR BIAS?

As part of the Triangle Bird Count, volunteers receive training on how to identify birds, and then they do a point-count survey. Just like Deja was doing when the angry woman interrupted her, these volunteers record every bird they see or hear from a specific spot during a specific time period. However, unlike with eBird, these volunteers cannot collect data wherever they feel like it. Instead, Deja and her collaborators select locations across the city ahead of time, to make sure all neighborhoods across the three cities are being sampled. Volunteers can choose from these pre-picked locations.

To check for bias in the volunteer eBird data, Deja has been comparing it to the data collected by Triangle Bird Count volunteers. Like many of the projects you've learned about in this book, Deja's research isn't finished. So far, though, she's finding that point counts at pre-picked locations that cover all parts of a city are a better way to measure the diversity of birds than eBird's free-for-all method. Before the Triangle Bird Count, there were areas in the cities Deja studies that had almost no data on birds. For example, in Raleigh and Durham, most of the eBird data comes from richer neighborhoods, leaving half of these cities unsampled by volunteers. While the Triangle Bird Count is still in its early years, its volunteers are already helping scientists learn more about the birds that inhabit Raleigh, Durham, and Chapel Hill.

Birds and culture

Human culture can have a huge influence on nature in cities. Take the black kites in Delhi, India. These medium-sized raptors do well in most urban areas, and can be found in Europe, Africa, Asia, and Australia. But their populations are extra-large in Delhi. Scientists have linked these kites' success to three things. First, Delhi's trees provide the perfect space for these birds to build nests. Second, Delhi has a lot of trash lying around, meaning lots of food for kites who will hunt as well as scavenge. The third reason? Religious tradition. Many Muslim and Hindu people in Delhi perform a centuries-old practice of throwing meat scraps into the air to feed kites! These offerings happen at regular times in the day, often causing hundreds of kites to gather. Without this extra food, kite populations might not be quite as large as they are today.

What do birds do for humans?

Just like all of the other living things mentioned in this book, birds provide valuable ecosystem services to people beyond just looking and sounding nice. Many birds act as pest control for our crops, eating insects or rodents that might otherwise cause damage. Scavengers like turkey vultures clean up animal carcasses. Some bird species are also important pollinators and seed dispersers.

SO, WHERE ARE BIRDS IN THE TRIANGLE?

Deja doesn't just want to use the data from the Triangle Bird Count to understand how bias affects the way we gather information on city birds. She also wants to use this information to understand where the greatest diversity of birds is in these cities, and what might influence where birds spend time in urban spaces. Like Chris Schell, Deja wants to see if the greatest areas of bird diversity are also the richest neighborhoods.

So far, the data Deja has collected doesn't suggest that the luxury effect exists for birds in Raleigh. She thinks this may be because most of Raleigh's neighborhoods have a lot of tree cover—not just the rich areas. This tree cover makes for good habitat all around. However, Deja is seeing that there are big differences in bird diversity in old versus new communities. Newer subdivisions have fewer bird species than ones that are more established, probably because the habitat has been recently disturbed, remodeled, and sometimes removed.

From redlining to environmental gentrification

We already learned historic practices like redlining and other forms of racial segregation have had an impact on who has (and does not have) access to biodiversity in some cities today. While it's important that we make all neighborhoods greener, if we aren't careful, processes like environmental gentrification may continue to prevent all city residents from having equal access to biodiversity.

Gentrification is a process where neighborhoods change as wealthier, often white, people and businesses move in. Neighborhoods undergoing gentrification are often those that were once low-income communities where people of color (Black, brown, Indigenous) often live. While gentrification brings money and resources back into communities, increases in rent may sometimes force poorer people to move to neighborhoods that lack services.

Environmental gentrification occurs when a large-scale greening project (like New York City's High Line) makes a neighborhood more attractive, increasing rent and home prices and making that area unaffordable for former residents. If we want to make sure that all communities have access to green space, but prevent environmental gentrification, it's important that we include neighborhood residents in the planning process and make changes gradually and at smaller scales.

In future, Deja hopes to compare the data from the cities in the Triangle Bird Count to urban areas like Tucson, Arizona, and Fresno, California, where other long-term programs are tracking bird populations. Together, the data from these projects and the volunteer-reported data from eBird will help us better understand what birds live in cities and where we can find them. Once we know this, we can begin to explore what features in cities (like tree cover, wetlands, or parks) birds seem to like, helping us to design urban areas that welcome birds.

Please keep your cats indoors

While many cat owners feel guilty about keeping their feline friends inside, indoor cats live longer and get sick less often than those that live outside. Keeping cats inside also keeps other animals safe. Even the most well-fed cats still have the instinct to hunt and kill birds, small mammals, and reptiles. Because domestic cats are not native to many areas where people keep them as pets, most local animals have not evolved the skills needed to avoid them. It has been estimated that they kill billions of birds and mammals worldwide, every single year. If you really do feel like your cat could benefit from outdoor time, consider getting them an outdoor enclosure that keeps them in and other animals out.

URBAN ECOLOGY CHALLENGE

Growing up in Chicago, Deja mostly encountered nature through the car window as her parents drove her around the city. Her favorite thing to do on these car rides was watch for birds. Deja loved learning the names of her local birds, and she wants you to do the same!

Get your notebook, check with an adult, and head out to your backyard or a local park. If you have some binoculars, bring those along, too (but don't worry, you'll still see lots without them). Take a look at the treetops. Can you find any birds? If you can't see them, can you hear them calling? If you spot a bird, write down what color it is and draw its shape in your notebook. Pay attention to what the bird is doing. Is it eating? Cleaning its feathers? Write down any behaviors you notice. If the bird is singing, write down what their call sounds like—or make a recording with a smartphone or other device.

Now you can take your notes home and do some research. Your local library likely has a field guide that will help you identify bird species common to your area, or you can look them up online. How many different types of birds can you identify in your neighborhood?

For an extra challenge, see if an adult will help you create an eBird account. Look for areas in your neighborhood that don't have any recorded data and see if you can go birdwatching there. You can then upload your observations to fill in gaps and help out scientists like Deja!

CHAPTER 8

A BIKE
TO BEAT THE HEAT

Why are greener cities better for people?

THINK BACK TO THE LAST TIME YOU WERE PLAYING OUTSIDE on a sunny summer day. When it got a little too hot, did you take a break in the shade of a tree? If so, I bet that shade felt pretty great. Nature has the power to improve our mental well-being and make us happier. But it also provides us with physical benefits, like cooling. Cities can get very hot, and this extreme heat can make people sick. It also means that we use air conditioners more to cool off buildings. All that extra energy use makes power outages more likely and contributes to climate change. We've known for a long time that trees and other plants help to cool cities down, but we didn't know how many trees we needed to create big cooling effects. At least, not until Carly Ziter showed up with her science bike.

WaIT, WHaT'S a SCIENCE BIKE?

Carly felt invincible tearing down one of Madison, Wisconsin's residential streets on her bicycle. Summer in Madison was off to a hot start. It was 27 degrees Celsius (80 degrees Fahrenheit) and Carly could feel the sweat dripping out from underneath her helmet. But she didn't care because it was working! It was finally working!

Carly pedaled faster. Two-story homes with perfectly manicured lawns and gardens zipped past her. Overhead, the afternoon sun peeked through the canopy of tall trees that shaded the street. Suddenly, Carly's joyous excitement was cut short by a blaring car horn. Snapping back to reality, Carly slammed on the brakes, barely stopping herself from flying over her handlebars. In her excitement, she'd almost run through a stop sign. As the car made its turn, Carly looked over her shoulder.

The small contraption she'd attached to the back of her bike was still whirring away quietly. This mobile weather station was measuring air temperature as she rode. Or at least she hoped it was measuring temperature. That was, after all, the purpose of today's test ride—to figure out if her science bike was actually doing what she'd designed it to do. Carly started pedaling again, but this time a little slower. After all, her science bike certainly wouldn't be collecting any data if she got into an accident.

Plant canopies

Plant canopies are the aboveground parts of plants. In forest ecology, canopy cover refers to the tops (or crowns) of large trees that cover the ground.

Carly's science bike includes a temperature sensor (covered by a solar shield to protect it from direct sunlight, which could cause incorrect temperature measurements), a GPS unit, and a data logger—all powered by a motorcycle battery.

As she rode, Carly thought back. It had been more than a year since she'd first dreamed up this contraption. She and Joel—her university's resident scientific instrument maker and an avid cyclist—had spent months building the small weather station and connecting it to her bike. Now was the moment of truth.

Carly turned into the science building parking lot and rushed her bike back to her office. Fiddling with a series of cords, she plugged her bike into her computer and waited for the data to download. Carly clicked the file and what she saw made her jump out of her chair. It had worked! The science bike had measured air temperature the whole ride. Slamming her office door shut, Carly ran down to the basement to tell Joel.

When is an urban heat island bad for people?

Hot days don't just make living in cities uncomfortable—they can be dangerous. Because of climate change, we are seeing more extremely high-temperature days in cities across the world. These hot temperatures can cause medical emergencies like heatstroke, especially in people who are very young, very old, or are suffering from other health conditions. Heat can also be risky for people who spend most of the day outside, like construction workers and landscapers. During hot weather, make sure to check on your friends and neighbors—especially if they do not have air conditioning. You can also check if your city offers public cooling centers that you can visit during extreme heat days.

WHAT MAKES CITIES SO HOT?

As Carly felt on her bike ride—and as you probably know if you've ever stood in a parking lot on a sunny day—cities are hot—much hotter than surrounding natural environments. This is called the urban heat island effect, and it's mostly caused by taking away vegetation. In areas that lack plants, the sun's energy is absorbed and then released by impervious surfaces like pavement and concrete. Picture that parking lot again—I bet you could feel the heat coming off the ground! In cities, heat also gets released by cars, air conditioners, furnaces, and other machines.

Impervious surfaces

These human-made land surfaces prevent rainwater from soaking into the ground. Examples of impervious surfaces include roads, parking lots, and the roofs of our buildings. These surfaces are often very dark and absorb more of the sun's energy than surfaces covered by plants—one of the reasons our cities get so steamy.

While cities are hot, plants help cool them down. Areas with large trees are cooler because of the shade those trees provide. Plants also cool the air around them through transpiration. When the sun hits plant leaves, water inside the leaves evaporates to help cool the plant down (just like our sweat cools us down when it's hot). The water that's released also helps to cool the surrounding air.

The many benefits of trees

Trees don't just help us cool our cities—they also provide other ecosystem services. Like other plants, trees create oxygen when they turn the sun's energy and carbon dioxide into food through photosynthesis. And trees provide habitats for many species of wildlife, like fungi growing on bark, or birds building nests in branches. Trees also provide us with tasty fruits like apples, oranges, limes, and coconuts.

WHAT CAN RIDING A BIKE TELL US ABOUT THE IMPORTANCE OF URBAN TREES?

Before Carly and Joel invented the science bike, scientists had been collecting temperature data throughout Madison and surrounding rural areas by putting temperature sensors that log, or store, information at the top of telephone poles. Once a year, graduate students like Carly would climb up these poles, get the sensors, download the data, and then put them back.

While this system worked well for understanding large-scale changes in temperature (and for students who weren't afraid of heights!), Carly didn't think it would be as useful for answering her questions. She needed to collect temperature measurements at smaller scales, and some of the areas she wanted to study didn't have any telephone poles to put a sensor on. Plus, buying hundreds of temperature sensors would have been very expensive!

To solve this problem, Carly decided to bring her temperature sensor to all the places she needed to go . . . on the back of her bicycle! After Joel helped her build it, Carly rode her science bike along 10 pre-planned routes (or transects) throughout Madison during the hottest part of the day and then again at night. The sensor on the back of her bike recorded temperature and her location every single second. At the end of each ride, Carly would transfer all that data from her bike to her computer.

Sponge cities

In China, cities like Beijing, Shenzhen, and Shanghai are solving another problem using native trees and plants: flooding. These cities are creating "sponge cities" by replacing concrete with wetlands, trees, green roofs, and gardens. All these plants soak up extra rainwater and reduce flooding. Some of this water is also being recycled for use in homes, and this added greenery helps to cool these cities down, too!

Carly rode her transects—each about 7 kilometers (or 4.3 miles) long—more than 80 times throughout the summer. That's almost 600 kilometers (372 miles), which would be like riding your bike from Montreal to New York City! Some of Carly's rides took her through the best parks in the city, full of mature trees. The kind of trees that seem to stretch all the way up to the sky, with branches perfect for climbing. Other rides took her through residential neighborhoods that had a mix of newly planted and middle-aged trees that might one day grow large enough to shade front yards. And some of Carly's routes took her through areas with no plants at all. These hot parking lots and city streets were her least favorite routes to ride.

HOW MANY TREES DOES IT TAKE TO COOL DOWN A CITY?

Carly's bike rides show that the cooling effects of trees are much stronger than we realized. On really hot days, trees cool the air down more than the pavement heats it up! This means that trees may be able to help us overcome the urban heat island effect—if there are enough of them. Carly's data shows us that almost half of a city neighborhood (about 40 percent) needs to be covered by treetops to get these big cooling effects. She's now excited to take her science bike to other cities across North America to understand how the number of trees we need to cool off urban areas may change in different climates.

Carly's work highlights that we can combat the warming effects in cities by planting trees. Because Carly figured out how much tree cover is needed to cool things off, her work is already being used to help design cities like London, United Kingdom, and Cambridge, Massachusetts. Covering 40 percent of a neighborhood with large, mature trees is a big task that will take time—many trees take a decade (but often longer) to grow that tall. But with time and teamwork, we can create cooler cities.

Coniferous or deciduous?

Deciduous trees are leafy trees that grow their leaves in the spring and shed them in the fall to help save water during the winter. Common deciduous trees in North America include oak, sugar maple, and birch.

Coniferous trees don't have leaves and instead grow needles. These needles, just like the leaves of deciduous trees, help trees photosynthesize (the process of turning carbon dioxide, water, and sunlight into energy). However, coniferous trees keep their needles all year long. Common North American examples include pine, cedar, and yew. Some coniferous trees, like the Bristlecone pine, can live to be up to 5,000 years old!

While both coniferous and deciduous trees provide humans with benefits, deciduous trees transpire more because of their larger leaves. This means they cool the air off more than conifers do.

URBAN ECOLOGY CHALLENGE

Growing up, Carly's favorite tree was a birch planted in her yard. Carly climbed this tree as a little girl and took family photos in front of it. One year, long after Carly had moved away, the tree fell down in a lightning storm. The tree had meant so much to Carly throughout her life that her dad packed up all the fallen branches and drove them to Carly's wedding. He surprised her by decorating the hall with them!

Carly wishes that more people thought of trees as individuals and got excited to learn about their unique traits. So, she wants you to learn about some of the individual trees that live in your neighborhood.

If you take a walk, chances are you can find at least five different types of trees. After checking with an adult, head outside and pick one of them. Is this a coniferous or a deciduous tree? Is the bark smooth or rough? Take a look at its leaves or needles. What shape do they have? How are they arranged? Write down or draw your observations in your field notebook. Can you use all of this information to figure out what species of tree it is? For an extra challenge, pick another tree close by and see how this individual is different!

CONCLUSION
But This Is Only the Beginning!

We share our cities with some amazing living things. The scientists you've met in this book are helping us learn more about how city living may be affecting those creatures, and how living so close to this biodiversity may be affecting us.

But I hope you've also learned some other important lessons:

- how we can creatively tackle problems in science (like Carly with her bike and Charlotte with her bug vacuum) . . .

- the importance of staying curious, because sometimes the answers to our questions may not be what we expect (like me with my bats and Kaylee with her rats) . . .

- that urban ecologists need the help of local communities to make their science possible (like Deja with her birds and Chris with his camera traps) . . .

- how sometimes animals and plants, just like people, need a helping hand (as Jesse showed us with her bears) . . .

- that small things can have a big impact on the health of our environments (as Rachel's work with invertebrates reveals) . . .

- how having nature around in cities makes us happier and healthier, and how everyone deserves to have equal access to this biodiversity . . .

- and, perhaps most importantly, that it is our job as humans to make sure that plants, animals, and insects can live alongside us in urban environments.

While we've covered everything from birds to bees and coyotes to bears, there is still so much urban ecology we haven't explored—like green roofs—the practice of putting plants on top of buildings. Green roofs can help cool cities off and provide more habitat for other wildlife. But what species survive best up high? How do climate and other factors affect plants on rooftops?

Light pollution is another big area of study for urban ecologists. All the extra nighttime light from our cars, buildings, and streetlamps can cause nocturnal animals to become disoriented and lose their way. And what about the ants you might have seen scurrying around your home? In cities like São Paulo, Brazil, scientists want to know how ants are handling the heat, while in Hong Kong, China, scientists are trying to track the spread of invasive ant species.

As our cities expand, it is more important than ever to understand the effects of urban development on our local ecosystems. The more that we know about how cities affect biodiversity, the better able we will be to design cities that help all species—including humans—lead healthier lives.

And before you go, don't forget! My urban-ecologist friends and I have given you some challenges to help you learn more about the plants, animals, and insects who may share your neighborhood. We hope you will complete all of these challenges. But don't stop there! Learn more about animals and plants not included in this book. Get involved in a local volunteer or community science project. Find out what you can do to help conserve the species that live in your city. Who knows, maybe one day you'll even grow up to be just like us—another urban ecologist discovering more about biodiversity in cities. But scientist or not, everyone living in cities can work to protect and help their local biodiversity. Even if the changes you're making seem small, when everyone makes small changes together, they can have a big effect.

ACKNOWLEDGMENTS

This book was written on the ancestral lands of the Haudenosaunee, Anishinabeg, Wendat, and Mississaugas of the Credit. Further, the natural-history information contained in these pages was collected on the traditional lands of other Indigenous peoples from across the world. I thank and pay my respects to these cultures and peoples for their stewardship of the land and the taxa that inhabit them. This stewardship has made my work as an ecologist today possible. My acknowledgment does not change the legacy of colonialism. However, I look forward to continuing to take personal steps toward reconciliation by speaking up against anti-Indigenous racism, donating to Indigenous-led organizations, and amplifying the voices of Indigenous leaders, scholars, creators, scientists, and people.

To my editor—Claire Caldwell—thank you for sticking with me through this entire process, even when my thesis writing delayed book writing. You've helped me make this into something I am incredibly proud of. Jesse Hildebrand, if it weren't for you, Claire might never have found me in the first place, so thanks for that.

This book would not have been possible without all the scientists involved. Jesse Popp, Carly Ziter, Charlotte de Keyzer, Kaylee Byers, Deja Perkins, Chris Schell, Rachel Giles, Rowshyra Castañeda, Charles Plaisir, and Elizabeth Carlen, thank you for sharing your knowledge, expertise, and personal stories with me. I owe special thanks to Chris for showing me that my science should not be separate from my social-justice work.

Much appreciation to my family and friends who began promoting this book before I even began writing it. Y'all never fail to amaze me with your support. And finally, Spencer Johnstone, your initial read-throughs of half-baked paragraphs and ideas were extremely helpful. I hope Logan enjoys reading this book as much as you did when he's old enough.

SELECT SOURCES

Introduction:
United Nations, Department of Economic and Social Affairs, Population Division. "World Urbanization Prospects: The 2018 Revision (ST/ESA/SER.A/420)." New York: United Nations, 2019.
https://www.un.org/development/desa/publications/2018-revision-of-world-urbanization-prospects.html.

Chapter 1:
Bat Conservation International. "Bat Houses."
http://www.batcon.org/resources/getting-involved/bat-houses.

Bat Conservation Trust. "National Bat Monitoring Programme."
https://www.bats.org.uk/our-work/national-bat-monitoring-programme.

Fenton, Brock M., and Nancy B. Simmons. *Bats: A World of Science and Mystery.* Chicago: The University of Chicago Press, 2014.

Patriquin, Krista J., Cylita Guy, Joshua Hinds, and John M. Ratcliffe. "Male and Female Bats Differ in Their Use of a Large Urban Park." *Journal of Urban Ecology* 5, no. 1 (2019): 1–13.
https://doi.org/10.1093/jue/juz015.

Visit Austin. "How to Experience Austin's Bats."
https://www.austintexas.org/things-to-do/outdoors/bat-watching/.

Chapter 2:
Byers, Kaylee A., Susan M. Cox, Raymond Lam, and Chelsea G. Himsworth. "'They're Always There': Resident Experiences of Living with Rats in a Disadvantaged Urban Neighbourhood." *BMC Public Health* 19 (2019): 853.
https://doi.org/10.1186/s12889-019-7202-6.

Centers for Disease Control and Prevention. "Diseases Directly Transmitted by Rodents." National Center for Emerging and Zoonotic Infectious Diseases, Division of High-Consequence Pathogens and Pathology. Page last reviewed July 5, 2017.
https://www.cdc.gov/rodents/diseases/direct.html.

Centers for Disease Control and Prevention. "Zoonotic Diseases." National Center for Emerging and Zoonotic Infectious Diseases. Page last reviewed July 14, 2017.
https://www.cdc.gov/onehealth/basics/zoonotic-diseases.html.

Gibbons, Ann. "Bonobos Join Chimps as Closest Human Relatives." *Science* website, June 13, 2012. https://www.sciencemag.org/news/2012/06/bonobos-join-chimps-closest-human-relatives.

Kark, Salit, Andrew Iwaniuk, Adam Schalimtzek, and Eran Banker. "Living in the City: Can Anyone Become an 'Urban Exploiter'?" *Journal of Biogeography* 34 (2007): 638–651. https://doi.org/10.1111/j.1365-2699.2006.01638.x.

Kirk, Mimi. "Urban Monkeys Are Too Chunky." Bloomberg CityLab, August 8, 2017. https://www.bloomberg.com/news/articles/2017-08-08/the-world-s-urban-monkeys-are-getting-too-fat.

Wilson, Don E., Russell A. Mittermeier, and Thomas E. Lacher, eds. *Handbook of the Mammals of the World*, Vol. 6, *Lagomorphs and Rodents I*. Barcelona: Lynx Edicions, 2016.

Wilson, Don E., Russell A. Mittermeier, and Thomas E. Lacher, eds. *Handbook of the Mammals of the World*, Vol. 7, *Rodents II*. Barcelona: Lynx Edicions, 2017.

Chapter 3:
BBC. "Plant Reproduction." BBC Bitesize. https://www.bbc.co.uk/bitesize/guides/zs7thyc/revision/1.

City of Toronto. *Bees of Toronto: A Guide to Their Remarkable World*. City of Toronto Biodiversity Series. Toronto: City of Toronto, 2016. https://www.toronto.ca/wp-content/uploads/2017/08/8eb7-Biodiversity-BeesBook-Division-Planning-And-Development.pdf.

Coulter, Lindsay. "How to Create a Pollinator-Friendly Garden." *Queen of Green*. David Suzuki Foundation website. https://davidsuzuki.org/queen-of-green/create-pollinator-friendly-garden-birds-bees-butterflies/.

Shea, Jessica. "Build Your Own Bee Hotel." Resource Library, National Geographic Society. Last updated July 9, 2012. https://www.nationalgeographic.org/media/build-your-own-bee-hotel/.

Chapter 4:
Hamr, Josef, Jesse N. Popp, Dorthy L. Brown, and Frank F. Mallory. "Problem Behaviour of Black Bears (*Ursus americanus*) in Central Ontario: The Effects of Hunting and Natural Food Availability." *Animal Biology* 65, no. 2 (2015): 151–161. https://doi.org/10.1163/15707563-00002467.

National Geographic. "American Black Bear." *National Geographic* website. https://www.nationalgeographic.com/animals/mammals/a/american-black-bear/.

Chapter 5:

The Grit City Carnivore Project.
https://gritcitycarnivores.org/.

Leong, Misha, Robert R. Dunn, and Michelle D. Trautwein. "Biodiversity and Socioeconomics in the City: A Review of the Luxury Effect." *Biology Letters* 14, no. 5 (May 2018): 20180082.
https://doi.org/10.1098/rsbl.2018.0082.

NSW Government. "Living with Kangaroos." Sydney: Office of Environment and Heritage, February 2011.
https://www.environment.nsw.gov.au/-/media/OEH/Corporate-Site/Documents/Animals-and-plants/Native-animals/living-with-kangaroos-100968.pdf.

Paz Gutierrez, Maria, Gene Demby, and Kara Frame. "Video: Housing Segregation in Everything." *Code Switch.* NPR, April 11, 2018. Video, 6:37.
https://www.npr.org/sections/codeswitch/2018/04/11/601494521/video-housing-segregation-in-everything.

Schell, Christopher J., Julie K. Young, Elizabeth V. Lonsdorf, Rachel M. Santymire, and Jill M. Mateo. "Parental Habituation to Human Disturbance Over Time Reduces Fear of Humans in Coyote Offspring." *Ecology and Evolution* 8, no. 24 (December 2018): 12965–12980.
https://doi.org/10.1002/ece3.4741.

The Schell Lab, University of Washington, Tacoma. "Grit City Carnivore Project."
https://faculty.washington.edu/cjschell/wordpress/gccp/.

Torres, Denise Freitas, Eduardo Silva Oliveira, and Rômulo Romeu Nóbrega Alves. "Understanding Human–Wildlife Conflicts and Their Implications." In *Ethnozoology: Animals in Our Lives*, edited by Rômulo Romeu Nóbrega Alves and Ulysses Paulino Albuquerque, 421–445. London: Elsevier, 2018.
https://doi.org/10.1016/B978-0-12-809913-1.00022-3.

Chapter 6:

Rutledge, Kim, Tara Ramroop, Diane Boudreau, Melissa McDaniel, Santani Teng, Erin Sprout, Hilary Costa, Hilary Hall, and Jeff Hunt. "Urban Heat Island." Resource Library, National Geographic Society. Last updated January 21, 2011.
https://www.nationalgeographic.org/encyclopedia/urban-heat-island/.

U.S. Geological Survey. "Evapotranspiration and the Water Cycle." USGS Water Science School.
https://www.usgs.gov/special-topic/water-science-school/science/evapotranspiration-and-water-cycle?qt-science_center_objects=0#qt-science_center_objects.

World Future Council. "Sponge Cities: What Is It All About?" January 20, 2016.
https://www.worldfuturecouncil.org/sponge-cities-what-is-it-all-about/.

Ziter, Carly D., Eric J. Pedersen, Christopher J. Kucharik, and Monica G. Turner. "Scale-Dependent Interactions between Tree Canopy Cover and Impervious Surfaces Reduce Daytime Urban Heat During Summer." *PNAS* 116, no. 15 (2019): 7575–7580. https://doi.org/10.1073/pnas.1817561116.

Chapter 7:
Government of Canada. "Microbeads." Last modified January 20, 2018. https://www.canada.ca/en/health-canada/services/chemical-substances/other-chemical-substances-interest/microbeads.html.

Moore, Charles. "Plastic Pollution." *Encyclopaedia Britannica Online*. Last updated October 15, 2020. https://www.britannica.com/science/plastic-pollution.

NOAA. "What Are Microplastics?" National Ocean Service, National Oceanic and Atmospheric Administration, U.S. Department of Commerce, March 30, 2020. Last updated February 26, 2021. https://oceanservice.noaa.gov/facts/microplastics.html.

Chapter 8:
Chapple, K., and T. Thomas. "Gentrification Explained." Urban Displacement Project, 2020. https://www.urbandisplacement.org/gentrification-explained.

eBird, The Cornell Lab of Ornithology. https://ebird.org/home.

Haffner, Jeanne. "The Dangers of Eco-Gentrification: What's the Best Way to Make a City Greener?" *Guardian*, May 6, 2015. https://www.theguardian.com/cities/2015/may/06/dangers-ecogentrification-best-way-make-city-greener.

Kumar, Nishant, Yadvendradev V. Jhala, Qamar Qureshi, Andrew G. Gosler, and Fabrizio Sergio. "Human-Attacks by an Urban Raptor Are Tied to Human Subsidies and Religious Practices." *Scientific Reports* 9 (2019): 2545. https://www.nature.com/articles/s41598-019-38662-z.

Mosco, Rosemary. "A Beginner's Guide to Common Bird Sounds and What They Mean." Birding By Ear. National Audubon Society, April 17, 2017. https://www.audubon.org/news/a-beginners-guide-common-bird-sounds-and-what-they-mean.

Conclusion:
Angilletta, Michael J. Jr., Robbie S. Wilson, Amanda C. Niehaus, Michael W. Sears, Carlos A. Navas, and Pedro L. Ribeiro. "Urban Physiology: City Ants Possess High Heat Tolerance." *PLoS ONE* 2, no. 2 (February 2007): e258. https://doi.org/10.1371/journal.pone.0000258

Graff, Steve. "Tracking Invasive Fire Ants in Asia." *The Scientist*, November 1, 2017. https://www.the-scientist.com/notebook/tracking-invasive-fire-ants-in-asia-30192.

INDEX